E-Safety for the i-Generation

E-Safety
for the
i-Generation

Combating the Misuse and Abuse of Technology in Schools

Nikki Giant

Jessica Kingsley *Publishers*
London and Philadelphia

First published in 2013
by Jessica Kingsley Publishers
116 Pentonville Road
London N1 9JB, UK
and
400 Market Street, Suite 400
Philadelphia, PA 19106, USA

www.jkp.com

Library of Congress Cataloging in Publication Data
Giant, Nikki, 1982-
E-safety for the i-generation : combating the misuse and abuse of technology in schools / Nikki Giant.
p. cm.
Includes bibliographical references and index.
ISBN 978-1-84905-944-2 (alk. paper)
1. Online etiquette--Study and teaching. 2. Internet in education. 3. Internet and children. I. Title.
TK5105.878.G53 2013
371.33'4--dc23
2012045943

British Library Cataloguing in Publication Data
A CIP catalogue record for this book is available from the British Library

ISBN 978 1 84905 944 2
eISBN 978 0 85700 774 2

Printed and bound in Great Britain

Contents

Part III Worksheets

Part IV Appendices

Part I

E-Safety for the i-Generation

Chapter 1

Introduction

Just a few short years ago the term 'e-safety' would have had no real relevance in our schools. Educators would not have thought to include e-safety in the curriculum. Parents would not have been concerned about their children's use of technology. Children and young people themselves couldn't have dreamed of the ways in which technology would form an integral part of their existence.

The twentieth century's explosion of technology has been unprecedented, and so complicit are we with the role of technology in our everyday lives that it is hard to remember a time when it did not exist. Many of us wonder now how we ever managed without a mobile phone, how business was conducted without email, how we managed to wait a week for holiday photographs to be developed.

It is within our lifetimes that this massive shift has taken place; a technological revolution that has changed our lives irreversibly. For most adults who remember life pre- and post-technology there is a feeling of appreciation for what is now possible with these technological advances, and perhaps even a sense of caution that technology cannot always be trusted. However, our young people have been born into a world where advanced technology already exists, and is not only normal but an expected right. The current generation of young children is the first not having experienced a world without information communication technology (ICT). For these so-called 'digital natives' (Prensky, 2001) the right and ability to use technology manifests itself in a myriad of ways, far outstripping the uses of most adults, with young people communicating, socializing, networking and creating through, with and because of technology.

With rights come responsibilities, and as we afford and at times, promote, the use of technology, including in the classroom, we often neglect to highlight the responsibilities that must come in tandem with these rights. The relative ease with which ICT can be abused and misused begs the question, if we teach our children how to use these tools, and freely give them access, who will teach them how to use them safely?

A 2010 report from the Kaiser Foundation in the USA found that young people aged 8–18 spend more than seven and a half hours each day using some form of media or technology, including TV, a games console or a computer, not including the hour and a half that youths spend texting, or talking on their phones. Aside from their time spent in school or sleeping, this equates to spending nearly every waking moment using some form of technology. The potential for bullying, access to inappropriate content, unsafe conduct, and general health and social risks related to technological over-use are naturally high.

It is becoming apparent that teaching e-safety must be offered in conjunction with teaching ICT and offering young people access to technologies. Wanting to keep our children safe has never been a higher priority, and it is crucial to note that their physical and emotional safety and their well-being extend beyond those dangers which are visible and tangible in the 'real world'.

How to use this resource

E-Safety for the i-Generation has been written to assist educators, in partnership with parents, carers and young people themselves, to understand students' use of technology and thereafter mitigate the risks of misuse and promote the responsibilities of safe and acceptable use, whether at school or at home.

Given that e-safety is a relatively new concept for many schools, *E-Safety for the i-Generation* has been designed to provide an overview of the subject, specifically addressing the use of technology by children and young people, and exploring the impact of unsafe or risky behaviour when using technology within a school environment.

This book explores the potential benefits and risks posed to young people by new technology, and defines an appropriate school response, including creating an e-safety policy, outlining staff and student codes of conduct, and implementing a comprehensive whole-school approach to e-safety that embeds positive, appropriate use of all forms of technology across the school community, including, but not limited to, within the curriculum.

The curriculum activities and worksheets explore the four themes of e-safety: Communication in the Digital Age, Being Safe, Netiquette and Cyber Bullying. Each activity can be used within an existing Personal Social Health Education or ICT curriculum, or the four themes of activities can be utilized to form a standalone scheme of work.

Chapter 2

E-Safety

What Does it All Mean?

Many adults will admit to having less knowledge about technology than their children, and certainly the way in which children and young people use technology is very different to adults. A report by the Pew Research Center in the USA found that three-quarters of teens now have a mobile phone, with as many as 58 per cent of 12-year-olds owning a phone, up from just 18 per cent of such teens as recently as 2004. Further, researchers found that 93 per cent of both teens and adults aged 12–29 go online, compared to only 74 per cent of all adults (Pew Research Center, 2010). A study conducted by the international consumer research specialist Intersperience declared that 65 per cent of the approximate 32 million smartphone users in the UK would declare themselves to be 'lost' without their phone (2012), while a 2011 Ofcom report into technology use found that 81 per cent of smartphone users have their phone switched on all of the time, even when they are in bed, with 40 per cent of teens admitting to using their smartphone after it woke them.

As technology becomes more commonplace, consumer use by people of all ages grows – adults are now far more likely to use social networking sites such as Facebook and Twitter, and more people own a smartphone today than ever before – once the ubiquitous business executive tool, smartphones and similar web-enabled 'smart' devices are now for the many, not just the few. But while adult use of technology is growing, it is often very different to that of young people. Adults over the age of 50 are more likely to use a desktop computer than a laptop or web-enabled device, and more likely to get their news in print form rather than online, with only a quarter likely to use a social networking site (AARP, 2010).

When exploring and developing a school response to e-safety it is important to recognize that some staff members' (and parents') awareness of the subject may be limited. It is likely that within your staff group some members will have never seen or used a social networking site, and may be at best a basic user of a computer. Undertaking a whole-school approach to e-safety should begin with a general staff training or information-sharing session to establish a shared level of understanding, ensuring that all members of staff are aware of why there is a need to address e-safety with students, parents and carers, and within the curriculum.

What is E-Safety?

E-safety relates to the safe and responsible use of information communication technology (ICT), including computers, the internet, mobile and communication devices, and technological tools that are designed to hold, share or receive information, for example mobile phones, digital cameras and pagers.

When using an electronic or technical product we are generally aware of the safety 'rules' that relate to how the item should be managed to avoid any physical harm coming to its user. This mostly can be deemed as common sense, and the ability to unconsciously misuse or abuse the technology to a worrying or dangerous degree is generally limited.

But when we consider the internet and other ICT, the safety rules seem non-existent or are certainly not promoted. The internet represents a vast network of billions of people, connected and accessible as a virtual world from the comfort of one's office desk or armchair. Perhaps it is the incongruence between the physical environment around us that we experience with our five senses – the familiarity and safety of our office or living room – that stands in such stark contrast to the conceptual 'reality' of the virtual world at our fingertips. So difficult it is to appreciate that we have access to almost the whole world in front of us, that we defer back to our immediate experience and 'forget' the potential of what cannot be seen, felt or sensed, but nonetheless still exists.

The difficulty for us to conceptualize what the internet and related technologies represent can lead us to be wary and distrustful, perhaps relying on our intuition, or at least our common sense to navigate our way through, particularly because as adults we can recall a time when these technologies did not exist. But with common sense usually comes a degree of maturity, and a sense of individual responsibility, as well as perhaps a moral appreciation of right and wrong. Generally these qualities are linked to age, and we do not expect children and young people to hold the same degree of maturity, responsibility and moral values as the adults around them.

However, when we consider that we are affording children (whom we know to be immature, unaware and without the mental capacity to rationalize and conceptualize future risks) access to technologies that we ourselves recognize as potentially dangerous, it is of no surprise that we see evidence of a lack of e-safety all around us. High-profile examples in the media of cases of sexual predators using the internet to groom and gain access to children are frightening, but in reality fairly rare, and it is the lesser, yet potentially as damaging, examples of unsafe behaviour when using technology that often go unrecognized.

With so many children and young people owning a mobile phone and having access to the internet it is too late and unproductive to deny our children and pretend the technology doesn't exist. The time has come to make explicit in our homes and classrooms not only the benefits of technology, but also the risks, and therefore the related responsibilities, to keep our children safe and ensure their well-being, in both the real and 'virtual' world.

Understanding the Terms

The growth of technology can make it difficult for the unseasoned user to keep up – the list of products, sites, terms, slang and acronyms can appear to be never-ending, often leaving many adults behind. The following is provided as an overview of the aspects of technology that children and young people regularly use, and it is advisable to get to know the technology first-hand by exploring it, for example setting up your own profile on a social networking site. This will provide you with a much better understanding of how it works and why young people may use it, as well as demonstrating potential risks.

Social Networking Sites
POPULAR EXAMPLES: FACEBOOK, TWITTER, PINTEREST

Social networking sites are generally free to join and very easy to access. Users sign up to the site and create their own profile to be shared with and seen by others. This will generally include information such as the user's name, hometown, educational and employment history, likes and dislikes, and photos, depending on the site's theme. The user then adds 'friends' (other users), giving them access to their profile information and allowing them to communicate with other users through the site, sharing information and photographs, for example. A whole breed of social networking sites have exploded, with Facebook and Twitter being the most commonly used. Other sites allow users to network around a particular theme or purpose, such as LinkedIn for business and career networking, or Instagram for those wanting to share images.

+ Great for keeping in touch and making contact with those in far-flung places or interested in a shared topic, getting an insight into other people's lives, sharing information such as photos instantly and easily.

− There is a trend, particularly among young people, to aim to add as many 'friends' as possible, meaning that users are potentially giving access to their personal information and photos to strangers or mere acquaintances. Some users are also unaware of how to keep their profile private (i.e. only their identified contacts can see it) which can result in their profile being seen by anyone, even those who are not users of the social networking site. This can create a potential for highly private information, such as an email address, home address and phone number (if added by the user to their profile), to be viewed by anyone.

Instant Messaging (IM)
POPULAR EXAMPLES: G-CHAT (GOOGLE MAIL), YAHOO CHAT, FACEBOOK CHAT

Instant messaging (or IM) is a tool to connect and talk instantly with anyone, via a computer or mobile phone with internet access. Users sign up with their email address and typically add contacts using other people's email addresses. If those people are also signed up to the IM service, users can communicate immediately in real-time by selecting a contact and typing a message. The messages are instantly displayed on the other user's computer, if they are also signed in to the service. Depending on the platform used, IM users can also chat via webcam (video link). Many social networking sites and other platforms have incorporated this technology now, such as Facebook and Skype; the latter has recently been announced to be replacing the popular MSN system.

+ It's a free and very easy way to keep in touch, particularly with those overseas, cutting down on expensive phone bills. Users can potentially have a number of private conversations (separate dialogue boxes open for each contact) at the same time, and it is easy to use IM to share photos and documents.

− As with social networking sites, the trend is to add as many contacts to your IM as possible, resulting again in the potential for strangers or acquaintances to access a user and have a 'private' conversation, potentially involving a webcam also. IM is often used as a tool to cyber bully, which is discussed further in Chapter 6.

Online Chat Rooms
POPULAR EXAMPLES: YAHOO CHAT

As the name suggests, online chat rooms allow users to chat, publicly or privately, with others over the internet through a dedicated website. Similar to IM, most chat rooms require users to sign up and the user selects a pseudonym to be known by, which is displayed in the chat room. Users can then have a public discussion (i.e. it can be seen by all other users of the chat room) or can elect to have a private conversation (i.e. a separate dialogue box is opened which only those invited can see). Lots of chat rooms and chat sites are centred on particular interests, such as music, and there are many aimed specifically at children and young people.

+ Chat rooms are generally free and easy to use and allow users to have real-time conversations. For those interested in a particular topic, such as a genre of music, chat rooms can be a great way to talk with others of like minds. Most reputable chat rooms for children and young people are highly monitored to negate any improper use.

− The potential for users to be drawn into inappropriate conversations on some chat room sites may be high, as many sites are unfiltered and unmonitored. Chat rooms can also be used to 'groom' children and young people, as the method of chatting can breed familiarity and confidence quickly. There is no way to know if the person you are chatting to is who they say they really are, and a photo or information offered can be deceptive to young people who may trust what they see and are told. Statistics present a worrying trend of young people meeting online contacts in the real world, often unaccompanied by others.

Gaming Devices with Internet Access
POPULAR EXAMPLES: PLAYSTATION, XBOX, NINTENDO DS

Gaming devices, such as the PlayStation and Xbox, are hugely popular, particularly with boys but increasingly with girls too. The games console is wired to a TV and games are generally bought separately, loaded into the console and viewed on the TV. As technology improves the trend is for consoles to have the ability to access the internet to allow players to play against others, potentially from anywhere across the world. Headsets allow users to talk to others as they play.

+ Games consoles are hugely popular, and some research points to gaming improving users' cognition and fine motor skills. Playing against real people through an internet connection can add more realism to games.

− Other research presents an opposing argument that games consoles can be highly addictive and overload users' senses, affecting concentration and encouraging somatic complaints. Many games are highly realistic and graphic, and although games are now age rated (i.e. games labelled as '18' cannot be bought by under-18s) many children have access to these graphic games, which can be highly violent and inappropriate.

Text and Picture Messaging

Nearly 91 per cent of people in the UK own a mobile phone (Ofcom, 2011), with the average person spending £439 a year on their mobile phone (Billmonitor, 2011), while in the USA 85 per cent of adults own cell phones with 72 per cent using the phones to send text messages (Pew Research Center, 2011).

A text message is a mini-email, sent instantly from one mobile phone to another. It is generally a cheaper way of communicating than by phone call. Picture messaging works in a similar way as most mobile phones now have inbuilt cameras, allowing pictures to be sent instantly from one phone to another for a low rate.

+ Cheap, easy and used by millions of people, text and picture messaging is a great way to communicate small bits of information and to share photos and images.

– Text messaging can be used as a tool to cyber bully, whereby threatening or harassing messages are sent. Additionally, a degrading or private image can be forwarded on to anyone, be passed from phone to phone, and can also be downloaded to the internet. Once an image has been forwarded in this manner it is impossible to retrieve it and it is potentially 'out there' forever.

Blogs and Vlogs

A blog is an online diary, and a vlog an online video diary. Those who keep a blog (bloggers) post regular information on the internet on a particular blogging platform, or on their social networking site. Like a regular diary, a blog or vlog can, however, be potentially viewed by anyone with access to the internet. Many famous people, such as singers and bands, have blogs or vlogs to stay in contact with fans and as a promotional tool.

+ Great for promoting yourself and sharing information about your life, getting it 'out there'.

– Many young people who have blogs or vlogs may not realize the impact of posting potentially private or intimate information about their life online. Blogs or vlogs can also be used as a way of inciting hate, degrading others or to promote dangerous or inappropriate views.

Why Is E-Safety Important?

The role of ICT in our schools has shifted dramatically within recent decades. It is now an integral part of the curriculum, and most children will enter school with a degree of proficiency in using ICT, rather than expecting to leave school with a basic understanding of how to type, create spreadsheets and use simple programmes, as for previous generations.

In this digital age it is clear that an understanding and aptitude in using technology will be vital in whatever future world of work or further education young people may embrace. Now, ICT is not only taught as a distinct subject, but features throughout the curriculum and school life as a whole. Whether used within art lessons for an animation project, as a research tool for writing a science assignment or creating a presentation for an English lesson, ICT is embedded throughout the school.

However, the practical and educational usage of the technology is completely surpassed by young people's private use, outside of the school gates. More young people than ever before have a profile on a social networking site, such as Facebook, which encourages users to network and connect with others, sharing information and images with their friends and contacts. A whole new wave of internet usage is emerging, navigating away from just viewing content to creating it. The shift from what was described as 'web 1.0' usage to 'web 2.0' describes the move towards an internet that is more personal and interactive. Websites encourage interaction from their viewers, by posting comments and adding thoughts and commentary to engage and promote buy-in.

Websites such as YouTube, which allows users to view and upload videos, permits the average person to be a contributor to the web, and share with a potentially worldwide audience. It is clear that today young people not only view content but they create it. Children and young people are now active participants in utilizing new technology.

A study conducted by Ofcom (2010) of media literacy in children and young people aged 5–15, found that:

- Only 1 per cent of 12–15-year-olds in the UK do not have home internet access.

  ◦ Half of 5–7-year-olds (49%), two-thirds of 8–11-year-olds (67%) and three-quarters of 12–15-year-olds (77%) have a TV in their bedrooms.

  ◦ Eighty-five per cent of parents trust their child to use the internet safely.

  ◦ Only 34 per cent of parents whose children are aged 12–15 are likely to be concerned about internet content.

The Physical, Social and Emotional Impact of Technology

While most parents, carers and educators can understand the rationale behind e-safety, understanding *why* children and young people can deliberately misuse the technology or be inadvertently found in a risky situation is a more difficult concept. Research conducted into cyber bullying suggests that perpetrators often don't fit the traditional stereotype of a school bully, or may even be victims of bullying themselves. With the technology affording a perceived sense of anonymity, there is perhaps an increased tendency to say things that one wouldn't say in the 'real world' (Smith *et al.*, 2008).

Communicating exclusively via the written word also presents additional clues as to why young people may misuse or abuse the technology. Face to face communication provides numerous non-verbal cues that relay vital information to the listener about the authenticity of what is being presented, and links to intuition and internal fear or danger responses. The emotional cues presented in a face to face exchange are extremely diminished when communicating only in the written word. For those who bully using technology, there can be a lack of understanding of the impact of their behaviour, and decreased empathy for the victim as they are unable to visibly observe the effects of what they are saying or doing to the other person.

The social skills gained from face to face communication and exchanges are quite simply missing to a large extent when communicating via technology. For any parent or teacher who has ever tried to decipher a child's text message, it is clear that with technology children speak a whole different language! Additionally, when exchanging in this way children's key social skills are not being developed, such as knowing when to talk and when to listen, how to reflect on social cues, body language and facial expression awareness, and understanding tone and intonation. This can lead children to become isolated from their peers in the real world or be placed at risk because of a lack of awareness about the information presented to them by someone dangerous or who is not to be trusted.

A study conducted by Carnegie Mellon University concluded that internet use leads to small but statistically significant increases in misery and loneliness and a decline in overall psychological well-being (DeAngelis, 2000). The appropriately named *HomeNet* project studied a sample of 169 people in Pittsburg, USA, during their first year or two online. The data showed that as people in the sample used the internet more, they reported keeping in contact with fewer friends. They also reported spending less time talking with their families, experiencing more daily stress, and feeling more lonely and depressed. These results occurred even though the study's participants stated that interpersonal communication was their most important reason for using the internet.

Eminent neuroscientist Baroness Greenfield warned that a 'sensory-laden environment' of computers could result in people 'staying in the world of the small child', with a potential link between a reduced attention span of children and the growing use of computers. Speaking in a BBC Radio 4 interview in 2008 she drew the link between the three-fold increase in children's use of the drug Ritalin (often used to treat symptoms of Attention Deficit Disorder) and the exposure of children to long hours of screen time, in front of computers, TVs, phones and gaming devices (BBC, 2008).

With this increasing use of the internet and related technologies in children as young as two, there is a debate among psychologists as to the prevalence of a psychological disorder associated with online use. Labelled by some as Internet Addiction Disorder (Goldberg, 1996), studies suggest the growth of addictive behaviour patterns among heavy internet users (Greenfield, 1999; Young, 1998). Research states that excessive use of the internet can result in personal, family and occupational problems, such as pathological gambling (e.g. Abbott, 1995), eating disorders (e.g. Copeland, 1995) and alcoholism (Cooper, 1995).

Researchers attest that prolonged use of the internet and other technology also affects children physically – research points to increased prevalence of obesity, reduced concentration and muscle pain (Barkin *et al.*, 2006). Robert Kerbs, a researcher at the University of California, found that the internet can have a negative impact on time management, resulting in internet addiction, neglect of school tasks and lower involvement in family activities (2008).

As children get older there are different concerns: increasingly it is reported that university admissions departments and job recruiters are using a search engine such as Google to search for information about their potential candidates and trawling their social networking sites for clues as to their suitability for their organization. Young people with few privacy settings on their social networking pages will proffer an open gaze onto their lives, including their photos, interactions with others and status updates. The drunken party, lewd comment or bullying remark can be all that stands between youth and future doors clanging shut.

Governments' Standpoints

The importance of tackling and promoting e-safety is becoming increasingly recognized at a governmental level, filtering down to local agencies and schools themselves. In the UK Becta, the government agency promoting the use of information and communications technology, was disbanded in 2010; however, the Department for Education (DfE) and Department for Business, Innovation and Skills (BIS) pledge to continue key areas of Becta's work, supported by charities and other local and national agencies. In the USA a range of governmental and non-profit organizations exist to support youth, parents and educators to tackle e-safety and cyber bullying, including the Federal Communications Commission, GetNetWise, the Internet Keep Safe Coalition, National Cyber Security Alliance and Wired Safety.

At the very least, schools are expected to put web content filtering software in place to keep students safe from inappropriate content. A white paper produced by the web security technology company Smoothwall states that 'the web filtering standard set by Becta should be considered as the technical minimum threshold for safe internet access for children and staff in education as no other implementable standard currently exists' (2011, p.1). Becta set an accreditation standard for filtering products or services, including a need for the product or service to block 100 per cent of illegal material identified by the Internet Watch Foundation (CAIC) List (Becta, 2012). The software should also be capable of blocking at least 90 per cent of inappropriate internet content in each of the following categories:

- *'Adult'*: content containing sexually explicit images, video or text, the depiction of actual or realistic sexual activity.

- *Violence*: content containing graphically violent images, video or text.

- *Race hate material*: content which promotes violence or attack on individuals or institutions on the basis of religious, racial or gender grounds.

- *Illegal drug taking and the promotion of illegal drug use*: content relating to the use or promotion of illegal drugs or misuse of prescription drugs.

- *Criminal skill/activity*: content relating to the promotion of criminal and other activities.

- *Gambling*: content relating to the use of online gambling websites or information relating to the promotion of gambling and gambling advice.

While at present there is no statutory demand on schools to specifically address and educate students on e-safety, it is perhaps only a matter of time. The UK Department for Education loosely advises on using mobile and wi-fi technologies in schools, stating that:

> while mobile devices can be used to support learning, caution is advised if using mobile phones (or other personal devices) in an educational setting. When considering their broader approach to safeguarding and e-safety, schools may want to consider the specific issue of mobile technologies and how they should be used. As part of this, they may need to consider what constitutes acceptable use of mobile phones in school by both staff and students and management issues related to this. (2012, p.6)

As more schools embrace the use of technology, such as Interactive Smartboards, digital cameras, video cameras and editing software, and iPads and other tablets, the need for comprehensive e-safety becomes even greater, not only to protect students but also staff and the school as a whole. From June 2012 Ofsted, the UK school inspection authority, will feature e-safety and cyber bullying as a part of school inspection criteria, with outstanding schools demonstrating that students feel safe in school and understand how to keep themselves and others safe, including when using technology (Ofsted, 2012).

In September 2008, a nationwide programme was rolled out by the US Federal Trade Commission to increase public awareness and educate citizens about promoting the safe use of the internet by children and young people across America. This was mandated by Congress through the Broadband Data Improvement Act (United States Code, 2008a), and created a collaboration between 30 non-profit organizations, industry groups and government agencies, including the Department of Education and Department of Homeland Security. The programme consists of an online portal, www.OnGuardOnline.gov, to provide information to parents and young people about safe online behaviour, with an accompanying guide for parents entitled *Net Cetera: Chatting with Kids about Being Online* (Federal Trade Commission, 2010).

From a school perspective, guidance about the teaching and promotion of e-safety and the creation of school e-safety policies differs from state to state. However, the Children's Internet Protection Act (CIPA) went into effect in April 2001, requiring elementary and secondary schools purchasing or using computers with internet access received at a discounted rate under the 'E-Rate' programme (a government programme that makes computers and other technology products and services more affordable for eligible schools and libraries) to submit proof of internet safety policies and technology in place to protect children and young people from online material that is harmful to minors, including pictures, images or files that depict, describe or represent offensive material, including nudity, an actual or stimulated sexual act or sexual contact (United States Code, 2000).

The law states that the school, school board, local educational agency or other authority with responsibility for administration of the school put in place a policy of internet safety for minors that addresses young people's access to inappropriate content, the safety of young people when using email and other forms of direct communication, hacking and other illegal activities by minors, and restricting children's access to potentially harmful materials through the internet. Schools must also have enforced adequate technology protection for computers used by monitors, such as filtering or monitoring software.

In addition to these requirements, an amendment to the Children's Internet Protection Act added the statutory language from the Protecting Children in the 21st Century Act (United States Code, 2008b) to include added statutory requirements for schools to meet under the E-Rate programme. Specifically, the Protecting Children in the 21st Century Act directs E-Rate applicants to certify that their internet safety policies (required by the Children's Internet Protection Act) include providing internet safety and cyber bullying education for students. This should include teaching students about appropriate online behaviour, including on social networking websites and in chat rooms (United States Code, 2008).

With the rise in cyber bullying also increasingly becoming an issue to be addressed by schools, and other forms of misuses of technology affecting school life, the proactive and pre-empting stance of creating effective e-safety policies and practices now is a prudent and judicious step, to be recommended to any school.

E-Safety and the Legal Framework

A number of aspects of the use and abuse of the internet and related technologies are now governed by civil and criminal laws. Educating students about e-safety should also include raising students' awareness of the potential consequences of their behaviour when using technology, and students and staff should be made aware of what activities could be deemed as criminal offences and know how and when to report inappropriate or illegal acts, content or contact.

There are a number of laws that will be relevant to incidents of technology misuse and abuse that you may wish to highlight to both students and staff alike. E-safety is a broad and wide-ranging subject that could relate to many aspects of the law, including data protection, malicious communications, harassment, grooming and sexual offences. Given the rapidly changing nature of the technologies and the growing number of incidents of technology abuse and misuse, it is worthwhile keeping abreast of the legal framework and checking on an annual basis what changes in law, governmental and educational policy will affect the teaching and promotion of e-safety and how school-based incidents should be dealt with. Professionals are advised to inform themselves regularly and use their judgement when approaching e-safety.

Chapter 3

The Core Messages of E-Safety

There are a number of key risks to using technologies, for adults and children alike, including:

- physical dangers

- sexual abuse

- bullying and harassment

- identity theft

- illegal behaviour

- exposure to inappropriate or unwanted content

- obsessive or addictive use of ICT

- copyright infringements

- viruses and spam.

These key risks can relate to the use of any forms of technology or participation in specific activities, including accessing websites and online content, in particular email, online chat rooms, social networking sites (SNS), instant messaging (IM), online gaming sites, and the use of mobile phones, digital media and games consoles.

Negating the key risks enables us to categorize into the positive promotion of three main themes: safe content, safe contact and safe commerce.

Safe and Appropriate Content

Safe content relates to ensuring that users, in particular children and young people, are protected from accessing or being exposed to inappropriate material or content, including that which is age-inappropriate or illegal, such as images or content which is violent, pornographic or overtly sexual, hateful or inciting hate, and abusive. In schools and other government managed or owned establishments, such as youth centres and libraries, access to inappropriate content is often generally restricted by blocking and filtering software and carefully monitored to diminish any risk. However, that is not generally the case for household or children's private computers, and certainly mobile devices, such as tablets and phones with inbuilt internet access, will have no such restrictions. Therefore, any efforts to ensure that children access safe content must also include educating students about how to personally manage and negate risks, in addition to installing monitoring and filtering software.

Safe content also includes protecting the user and the technology from security risks, such as viruses, spam, adware and spyware, which can be potentially damaging to the computer, the user's account (e.g. email account) and potentially allow others access to sensitive or private information for inappropriate or illegal gains.

Educating children about accessing safe and appropriate content is clearly not just about ensuring young people cannot access what is deemed to be inappropriate. Children need to become discerning viewers and users to build their own skills of acumen and to develop the responsibility to choose what to search for, watch and engage with. 'Content' is not limited to online material, but also includes that which children may be subjected to in everyday life, either unwittingly or intentionally, such as violent, aggressive and overtly sexual video games, TV shows and films, magazines and other literature. Access to these forms of content may go completely unnoticed by parents and carers, or may even be allowed and encouraged, such is the perceived normality of many games, shows and movies. The level of violence in some video games may be extreme, and yet the game may only warrant a rating of age 12 or older, deeming it to be acceptable for young people to play.

Anderson and colleagues found that 'research on violent television and films, video games, and music reveals unequivocal evidence that media violence increases the likelihood of aggressive and violent behavior in both immediate and long-term contexts' (2003, p.81). A study published in the *Journal of Adolescent Health* found that 'adolescents who are exposed to more sexual content in the media, and who perceive greater support from the media for teen sexual behavior, report greater intentions to engage in sexual intercourse and more sexual activity' (L'Engle *et al.*, 2006, p.186).

Safe and Appropriate Contact

The internet and related technologies offer unrivalled access for communication and contact with potentially millions of people all over the globe, easily and instantly. This presents a risk when contact is unwanted, or is abusive, misleading or dangerous.

It is widely understood that face to face communication is conducted not only through the spoken word, but through tone, intonation, body language and other non-verbal cues that alert participants to potential discrepancies, incongruencies or dangers. Virtual communication, however, often asks participants to make a judgement about the content by relying solely upon the words with which they are presented. This can be particularly difficult for children and young people with less maturity, awareness of risk and connection with their intuition or an inner sense of right and wrong.

Various forms of technology can be used to make harmful or inappropriate contact, such as through text message, IM, email and in online chat rooms, where users can speak to each other instantly and privately in 'real time'. Risks include the danger of adults making contact with children and young people for sexual gratification or grooming, the physical dangers of meeting online 'friends' in the real world, and cyber bullying, whereby technology is used as a method of harassment, discrimination and bullying of another.

The 'Chatwise, Streetwise' report from the Internet Crime Forum (2000) suggests that incidents of adult sex offenders meeting children online and gaining their trust are increasing in both the UK and USA. More than one third (38%) of all rapes recorded by the police in England and Wales in 2010/11 were committed against children under 16 years of age, with teenage girls aged between 15 and 17 reporting the highest past year rates of sexual abuse (Home Office, 2011).

Young people who meet online contacts in the real world are placing themselves in danger of being harassed, threatened, groomed by a paedophile or even subjected to sexual assault or rape by a person who may not be as they appeared online. Young people are in particular danger of becoming victims to these kinds of violent crimes when they lack the awareness to question the authenticity of the information they are presented with online.

A young woman who may believe she is meeting a local girl of her age after getting to know her online may find herself in a dangerous situation with a man who can easily overpower and attack her.

Safe and Appropriate Commerce

The advent of the internet has changed the world of business irrevocably and now a huge proportion of commerce is conducted through the internet. Many of us engage in online shopping, paying to download files, using internet banking and other such forms of online commerce, and recognize the ease with which business is conducted over the internet. The technology industry in itself represents billions of dollars of sales, as people rush to buy the latest laptop, smartphone, tablet and gaming device as they are released.

Children and young people are just as likely to be the targets of online advertisers or susceptible to unsafe or inappropriate commercial activities , such as using premium rate services on mobile phones, registering personal details on commercial websites, using parents' credit card details to purchase items over the internet and downloading files illegally, such as music albums.

Educating children and young people about the financial and commercial implications of using new technology and reducing dangerous or reckless use is a key aspect of teaching and promoting e-safety. Researchers state that there is 'growing criticism over ways in which children's rights to privacy may be violated by online advertising and unfair or deceptive practices' (Livingstone, 2003, p.16).

Exploring the Risks Further

Physical Dangers

- These are potentially posed by meeting online 'friends' in the real world or people who may not be who they say they are, and therefore putting oneself at risk of physical harm.

- Threats to safety and well-being are also made by others through the use of technology (harassment or cyber bullying).

Sexual Abuse and Exposure to Inappropriate Content

- Children viewing sexually explicit or age-inappropriate material inadvertently (e.g. through 'pop-ups' or by accidentally accessing sites).

- Children and young people accessing sexually explicit or age-inappropriate material by their own admission where limited or no filtering software is in place.

- Sexual harassment through technology (e.g. receiving unwanted or abusive phone calls or text messages of a sexual nature).

- Blackmail, threats, or extortion of a child or young person to engage in sexual acts or sexually explicit communication (e.g. a sexually explicit conversation in an online chat room).

- Grooming of a child or young person using technology by an adult for sexual gratification including the potential to meet and physically and sexually abuse a child or young person and/or engage in paedophilic acts.

Cyber Bullying and Harassment

- Explored further in Chapter 6, cyber bullying is the repeated harassment, degradation or abuse of another through or with technology. There are seven forms of cyber bullying – via text message, phone call, pictures/videos, email, online chat rooms, social networking sites, and websites in general (e.g. hate or bashing websites).

- A child, young person or adult can also be harassed through and with technology. This differs from bullying, which by its nature is repetitious and results in a perceived imbalance of power between victim and perpetrator.

- However, some forms of harassment to adults which may be a criminal offence are likely to be deemed as cyber bullying in a school setting.

Identity Theft

- Identity theft is becoming all too common as our personal details are more often required and held by businesses, organizations and agencies, with, and at times without, our knowledge.

- Identity theft relates to aspects of a person's identity being 'stolen' and used by someone else for personal gain and/or criminal activity.

- Personal information such as a name, address, date of birth, email address or in more serious cases, bank details or personal passwords are then used to build a 'picture' of someone so that another person can assume their identity or gain access to sensitive or private information.

Illegal Behaviour

- Laws exist in both the UK and USA, and elsewhere around the globe, that restrict the way in which music can be downloaded, copied or shared. In the USA, 'Federal law provides severe civil and criminal penalties for the unauthorized reproduction, distribution, rental or digital transmission of copyrighted sound recordings' (Title 17, United States Code, 2012 Sections 501 and 506). The USA was the worst offender for illegal downloading and sharing of music files in 2012, with 96,868,398 total shares. The UK was the next worst offending nation, with 43,314,568 shares (Musicmetric, 2012). Despite the laws in place many people still engage in this behaviour knowingly or unwittingly.

- The internet is also a huge source of income for criminal and illegal behaviour; for example, it can take just minutes to set up a bogus website and begin to 'sell' a product or service to a potentially worldwide audience.

- There is the potential for children and young people particularly to be duped into engaging in illegal activities through the use of technology or becoming the victims of crime.

Obsessive or Addictive Use of ICT

- As more and more of us use technology in our everyday lives, such as computers, mobile phones and gaming devices, the more reliant we can become upon them.

- Increasingly children as young as two or three years old have access to home computers, the internet and gaming devices such as XBoxes or PlayStations.

- Studies show that those with high usage of the internet and related technologies report becoming withdrawn, lonely, depressed and isolated.

Copyright Infringements

- The internet provides a wealth of information that could easily outweigh that contained in any library in the world. The benefit for helping and enhancing research projects, homework or assignments is obvious, but as with downloading music, the same copyright laws apply if a person's intellectual property is infringed. There is also the concern that not all of the information presented on the internet is accurate and reliable.

Viruses and Spam

- A computer virus could be described as a technological 'disease' that can potentially destroy its host, resulting in damaged or lost information or even the destruction of the technology itself. Viruses can be inadvertently or intentionally released into a computer by a corrupt file, a piece of software or via the internet.

- Spam is described as unwanted information, received from companies or individuals, e.g. via email or text message, selling goods or services or displaying inappropriate content.

It is important to note that while there are real and present dangers, the tools themselves are not dangerous, just as a car isn't dangerous until someone reckless gets behind the wheel. Because the internet and related technologies can seem so vast and complicated to understand, and because they represent a world of the unknown, there may be a danger that we consider the technologies to be risky, and therefore distrust them and create a sense of fear that prohibits our use and makes us wary of allowing our children access also.

Given the implications and potential risks, as discussed in this chapter, this is an understandable and natural reaction. Protecting our children from harm is paramount, and we aim to shelter them from the world as much as is possible. The internet, potentially representing the whole world in its entirety – good and bad – can be seen as an open portal into the unknown, and one that young people are keen to embrace.

It is a fact of life that children will have access to these technologies, whether we like it or not, and as adults our awareness of the potential risks and dangers is a first step to ensuring children's use is safe and responsible. However, we must balance this – as parents and educators – with an understanding of the important role of technology and the great advancements it offers. These technologies offer us instant methods of connecting with others, sharing information, researching, exploring and so much more, and are a wonderful teaching and learning tool that push the boundaries of the classroom, enhancing students' schooling experiences.

The technologies cannot be denied, and although we deny access to websites deemed inappropriate in schools and ban mobile phones this does not protect children and young people when they leave through the school gates; neither does it afford them with an understanding of what we are trying to protect them from, why, and how to protect themselves.

Just as a car isn't dangerous in itself, and indeed is of great value to those who wish to travel, technologies such as the internet are similarly so. Would we consider letting someone get behind the wheel having never driven before? Or would we first strive to educate them about how the car works, impress upon them the responsibility they hold in being a driver, and highlight the potential dangers, as well as the benefits, the open road may yield?

Is It a School Issue?

Many schools have found themselves in the precarious position of dealing with issues of unsafe or inappropriate behaviour that occurred when students used technology outside of the school grounds or school hours. It is most definitely a grey area as to whether a school should intervene and there is no clear line from a government or statutory standpoint.

While some schools simply refuse to deal with any incidents of behaviour that occurred outside of school hours, instead referring parents to the police or other statutory agencies, it is worthwhile noting that the role of teachers and schools is to educate young people, and children who are in any sort of physical, emotional or social pain may not be able to learn. A young person who has suffered a sleepless weekend after being tormented by cyber bullies will be unlikely to be in the best position to learn come Monday morning. A student who sent a sexually provocative picture to a boy which was subsequently forwarded throughout the school community may feel she can never return to school again.

Children cannot retain information, reason, debate, actively participate in classroom discussion, or cognitively engage to any great degree when they are emotionally charged. Daniel Goleman, the pioneer of emotional literacy, explains how high stress situations and strong emotions, such as fear or anger, create an 'amygdala hijack' whereby the emotional part of the brain which regulates the fight or flight response, the amygdala, feels threatened. The amygdala can 'hijack' the rational brain, sending a rush of stress hormones flooding throughout the body (Goleman, 1996).

It is for each school to decide upon the extent to which they will be involved in issues of e-safety and cyber bullying that occur outside of the school grounds, but governors or school board members and staff should remember that they have a duty of care, by law, towards their students.

Having a preventative e-safety programme in place, such as awareness-raising sessions, a comprehensive curriculum and written and online information available, should help to stem the flow of incidents and move schools from a reactive position to a proactive stance.

Chapter 4

Sex and Technology

It has long stood true that 'sex sells' and in today's world we are literally bombarded with sexual connotations, imagery and language. Sexuality and sexualized images are used to sell everything from cars to soft drinks, and anything else in between. Such is the pervasiveness of sex, sexualization and sexual imagery in Western society that many of us fail to even notice the often highly provocative, revealing or even degrading tactics used to portray men and women in advertising, TV, films, music videos, and in print and online media. This pervasive sexual culture is what Reg Bailey coined as 'the wallpaper of children's lives' in his report of an independent review into commercialization and sexualization of childhood, commissioned by the UK Department for Education in 2011 (DfE, 2011).

Bailey writes, 'The increasing number of media channels through which we receive [sexual] messages mean that we are under ever-increasing exposure to sexualised content and imagery. Sadly, some parent contributors even felt that there is 'no escape' and, for children, no 'clear space' where they can simply be themselves' (2011, p.23).

Young people, particularly, may be even more au fait with the images that surround them on a daily basis. They have been born and raised in a sexually charged world, with a society that often appears to dictate a need to appear mature and sexually ready from an increasingly young age. Recent media outcries by parents, educators and campaigners against the sexualization of children have begun to bring the issue to the wider public's attention. Concerns have been raised over an array of adult or inappropriate services and products marketed to children, such as shops selling thongs and push-up bras to under 12s, girls' dolls plastered with makeup and looking overly sexual, and the rise in birthday 'cocktail' parties, limousine rides, and makeovers marketed to girls as young as five. The increasing marketing to young children, and their growing consumerism with particular reference to adult-appropriate products, has been termed 'corporate paedophilia' by some, such is the depth of feeling of the negative impact of these business practices.

The development of our sexual being and individual sexuality is a natural part of growing up, as is the process of puberty giving way to a person's sexual discovery and romantic relationships. Healthy sexuality is an important aspect of physical and mental maturity that can strengthen a person's social, emotional and physical relationship with a consenting partner, with the correct guidance, knowledge and support. Sexualization, however, is the imposition of adult sexuality on to children and young people before they are capable of dealing with it, mentally, emotionally or physically (Papadopoulos, 2010). The American Psychological Association states that:

> sexualization occurs when a person's value comes only from his or her sexual appeal or behavior, to
> the exclusion of other characteristics; a person is held to a standard that equates physical attractiveness

(narrowly defined) with being sexy; a person is sexually objectified – that is, made into a thing for others' sexual use, rather than seen as a person with the capacity for independent action and decision making; and/or sexuality is inappropriately imposed upon a person. (APA, 2010, p.1)

The Report of the APA Task Force on the Sexualization of Girls (2010) states that sexualization can create self-objectification, whereby a young woman learns to think and treat her own body as an object of desire, defining her own needs and state of being as synonymous with that of young men's. She learns to treat herself as an object to be viewed, judging her value on her appearance, inevitably leading to low self-esteem, a lack of self worth and a lack of self respect. Self objectification has also been linked to poor sexual health and reduced sexual assertiveness in young women (Impett, Schooler and Tolman, 2006).

Sexualization and the early onset of engaging in sexual relationships can be damaging for young people, physically, socially and emotionally, with identified links to common mental health problems, such as eating disorders and depression (Ward, 2004). For young women in particular the conflicting need to appear available and sexually ready, but not be deemed a 'slut' by her peers, can lead to ostracism, relationship breakdown and bullying. A fine line is often walked for girls who don't want to be labelled as childish, or even an 'inexperienced virgin', while not gaining a reputation for promiscuity.

The sexualization of children and young people is a growing theme of research and debate, as more parents, educators, psychologists and academics acknowledge the impact of the 'drip drip' effect of a constant bombardment of sexual imagery and messages. But this sexualization of young people doesn't just affect girls – boys are just as likely to be targets of sexualized imagery and stereotypical perceptions of what a twenty-first century male should look and act like. As girls rush to appear more mature and sexually ready, boys similarly may feel pressured to play the role of the masculine, sex-mad and dominant male, so often depicted in popular teen culture.

While concerning, the issue of youth sexualization is not the main premise of this book. However, it is important to note the clear link between sexualization, sexually related risky behaviours and technology. The media, often accessed through technology, is the broadcasting channel through which the sexualization of young people will begin, compounded by other forms of print media, such as magazines. As young people are now constantly surrounded by technology, both the subtle and the explicit messages are a constant feature of life. Most of us cannot escape the continuous slew of sex.

The channels through which young people learn about sex, connect with a potential romantic partner and engage in flirtation and sexual acts, to some degree, are also increasingly technology based. The UK Family Planning Association states that children and young people 'learn about sex and relationships from both formal and informal sources. These include family, friends, the media, school and other educational settings, youth clubs, and from health professionals. These sources vary in their accuracy and many young people fail to obtain the information that they need about sex, relationships, contraception and sexually transmitted infections (STIs)' (2011, p2). The media is increasingly a main source of young people's knowledge about sex, often contributing to distorted views, stereotypes and inaccurate messages about sex, sexuality and relationships. The rise in young people viewing pornography, often on a home computer or handheld device, compounds these inaccuracies and faulty perceptions, leading to concerns about the normalization and increased consumption of pornography. There is a growing sense of social legitimacy about what was once a less popular, undercover behaviour. Australian researchers found that widespread access to technology has increased young people's consumption of pornography, with 'significant' proportions of young people exposed (Flood, 2009). In a 2006 study of 13–16-year-olds in Australian schools, 93 per cent of males and 62 per cent of females had seen pornography online (Fleming et al., 2006).

A paper produced in Australia by the Domestic Violence Resource Centre Victoria (DVRCV) highlights the negative impact pornography can have on young people's awareness and understanding of healthy sexual and romantic relationships. They state that 'porn has become a central mediator of young people's sexual understandings and experiences. Young people are exposed to porn at unprecedented rates. Many young people discover porn before they've encountered sex' (DVRCV, 2010). Additionally, research studies point to young women internalizing the messages of porn (Zwartz, 2007), creating an inaccurate and flawed insight into what sex with a partner entails, and compounding gender inequalities and stereotypes, with girls and young women often perceived as submissive objects for male domination and gratification. In a school environment this can lead to sexually inappropriate behaviour between students, sexual harassment and even the sexual exploitation of young people.

Added to the complex implications of this interplay between technology, pornography and young people is the issue of youth representing themselves as sexual commodities through and with technology, such as on their social networking sites and profiles on other platforms. This negative self-representation can also be a conduit for personal and social problems, many of which may end up in schools' hands. Young people may use their online profiles to experiment with their sexual identity and promote 'self-commodification' (Stern, 2006), whereby teens will display provocative images, messages and sexual content to communicate messages about themselves, such as promoting their beauty or sexual readiness. This content may be as subtle as publicly 'liking' a certain TV show, celebrity or icon, such as the ubiquitous Playboy bunny image, or posting comments about themselves or others.

Posting provocative or sexually loaded images of oneself on a social networking site can have dual results – attracting positive male attention, and negative female attention. Girls can often find themselves to be the unwitting recipients of bullying and abuse from other young women, or sexual harassment and sexually inappropriate responses from young men. Allowing the images they post to be commented upon, rated and shared further helps to create a sense of being a sexual commodity as opposed to a real person. Young women – and men – can quickly gain a reputation in a school and community, and often wider afield with the online web of connectedness, through the persona and information they present on their profiles and in other communication. A reputation for being a slut, tart, frigid, easy, gay and a wealth of other labels can leave young people branded for years to come and ultimately feeling isolated and unpopular.

With the prevalence of young people owning web-enabled smartphones and laptops or tablets for their own private use, the ability to communicate openly with anyone is a 24/7, free affair. Indeed, it appears that for today's youth, romantic relationships are conducted, at least initially, via technology. Text messages, social networking sites and other forms of instant, non-face to face contact are often the communication method of choice for young people.

This presents a worrying trend. Communication that is not conducted face to face creates a sense of distance, both in a physical and emotional sense. What one may never say or do in front of another person becomes acceptable, or even to be encouraged, with the virtual distance between computer or mobile phone screens. Cyber bullying and 'sexting' – the act of sending a sexual message or picture – is becoming increasingly common. In the UK it was found that one in three teenagers had received 'sexually suggestive' messages (Cross *et al.*, 2009). According to US research, one in five teenagers have engaged in sexting (NCMEC, 2009). A quantitative analysis of 700 MySpace profile pages, a once highly popular social networking site, found that 59 per cent of young respondents had included pictures of revealing sexual poses on their profiles, with 28 per cent of boys and 17 per cent of girls displaying partial frontal nudity. A frighteningly high 6 per cent of girls had uploaded a profile picture displaying full nudity (Pierce, 2007).

Sexting is the act of sending an image or message of sexual content or engaging in a sexual act through instant communication, often by text message. Sexting can range from heavy flirting with sexual connotations via message, to the sending of naked images. A conversation can quickly escalate for the uninitiated young person from harmless flirting to engaging in the sending of images or video that cannot ever be retrieved. Most young people are completely unaware of the permanence of such images – as easy as they are to delete from the sender's phone or computer, once sent, they can be instantly forwarded on to someone else, uploaded online, printed or otherwise distributed. Once an image or video is posted online it is virtually irretrievable forever. Any one of the billions of people around the world with a computer and internet access can download the image, copy, re-upload and potentially digitally alter or edit it.

An added concern for parents and educators alike is the legality of young people distributing or requesting explicit or nude images of girls under the age of sexual consent. Recent high profile cases have resulted in young men being placed on the Sex Offenders register – a chilling consequence to what may have started as a 'harmless' bit of fun.

Perhaps sexting is just simply the process of young people experimenting with sex and their sexuality as generations have done so before, albeit it in the communication form of the day. The physical, social and sexual development of young people is often a bone of contention for adults who wish for their offspring to remain children for just a little longer. But the explosion of technology and new media is simply unprecedented. Even if it is 'same story, different time' it must be acknowledged that the nature of the internet and instant communication creates a much more visual, public method of personal representation, the likes of which have never been seen before. While this can undoubtedly be positive, helping to showcase people's thoughts, ideas, causes and more, for young people who find themselves regretting their online behaviour, the repercussions of sexting and other online activity can be devastating. Recent reports of teen suicide have been attributed to acts of sexual engagement using media that seemed innocent enough at the time, but haunted youths until they felt there was only one way out.

Many adults feel that young people are not ready to engage in sexual activity, and certainly each person's maturity and readiness for romantic and sexual relationships will occur at a different time. Technology, coupled with the general sexualization of children and young people, may expedite this process, as more teens feel pressured into appearing, engaging and communicating sexually by peers and society. While young people may be physically ready to engage in sexual acts, often the emotional readiness is far from developed, coupled with a lack of reasoning and forethought. The pre-frontal cortex – the part of the brain which regulates behaviour and judgement – is not fully formed until around age 21, which explains why often children and young people are not able to visualize and conceptualize possible outcomes to understand the future repercussions of their behaviour.

The Role of Parents

Many parents feel that children are growing up too quickly, too early, yet feel powerless to stem the flow of external and internal pressures to which youth are constantly subjected, that dictate a need to grow up sooner than ever. Indeed, parental actions may even contribute to the sexualization of young people and their access to sexual content: parents may feel pressured to buy their children the latest products, even if they are inappropriate, such as too-adult fashions, or to 'keep up with the Joneses' by giving even young children access to internet-ready devices, such as smartphones, tablets, gaming devices and TVs, without providing the safety tools and awareness.

Parents can be completely unaware of their children's behaviour, with young people finding ever-increasing ways to outsmart adults whose technological understanding falls far short of their own.

Smartphones have access to 'app stores' where thousands of applications can be downloaded – often for free – with everything from mobile banking to newspapers accessed through apps. Parents who pay their children's smartphone bills might feel encouraged to find a lack of text messages sent (presumably indicating that their child has not been 'up to no good'), whereas many youths know how to access one of the dozens of apps that allow for free mobile-to-mobile text and picture messaging, never showing up on a bill, despite how many messages are sent. BlackBerry phones have their own version of this – BlackBerry Messenger (BBM) is BlackBerry's own application that allows for users to send free messages from BlackBerry to BlackBerry phone. An exchange of messages is possible to a single person or to multiple people via discussion groups, and users can additionally send pictures, audio recordings, files and a location on a map.

Schools, Sex, and Technology

Clearly parents have a role to protect and inform their children about the potential dangers and responsibilities of being online and using technology – at the very least having open and honest conversations about the repercussions of engaging in sexualized communication with their peers. But as with many personal and social issues, it appears that to some extent the onus may fall to schools to fill in the gaps left by parental discussion and guidance with regard to issues relating to sex and technology.

The growing use of social networking sites, smartphones and other online platforms by children and young people puts them at risk of sexualization, sexual violence and even paedophilia. Any issue affecting a child's well-being is a potential child protection issue, which if brought to the attention of school staff should be dealt with as such. A report of a student being targeted in a chat room by a sexual predator should be dealt with just as if the initiation occurred offline. Schools have a duty of care to students, and a legal obligation to report any issues concerning safeguarding. It may be a useful exercise to check whether your school child protection or safeguarding policy mentions technology-related risks. Training front-line support staff (particularly those who respond to student issues on a daily basis) to understand the risks of technology use is also crucial.

It is clear that schools are increasingly finding themselves dealing with the fall-out of young people's sexualized online behaviour, including sexting, with even young schoolchildren reportedly engaging in sexual acts and communication via phones and the internet. Being aware of the potential for problems being presented in our classrooms and school hallways will help us as educators to better support students, and mitigate the risks of problems occurring in the future.

While school staff cannot control young people's behaviour outside of the school grounds, or that which is conducted unbeknown to staff, each adult has a role to play to ensure that bullying, peer pressure, sexual harassment and sexual violence do not occur. It is advisable that students are not allowed to use mobile phones during the school day, and clear sanctions should be outlined for those who choose not to follow school rules in this regard.

Chapter 5

E-Safety at Home

While schools have a clear role to play in teaching young people about safe online behaviour, e-safety education must begin at home. Most families have at least one computer in the home, and many young people have smartphones and other internet-ready devices, so the likelihood is that most incidents of unsafe and inappropriate behaviour using technology will take place out of school time. With an ever-bulging curriculum it is unfair and inappropriate to expect schools to be the sole proponent of e-safety messages. Parental support and families' own education about e-safety will ensure a consistent message to youth, and will avoid incidents of cyber bullying and inappropriate behaviour being brought into school.

de Haan, Duimel and Valkenburg (2007) found that parents remain physically present during children's internet usage in about 30 per cent of families, while the majority rely on filtering software, or on checking the history of the internet browser (Beebe *et al.*, 2004; Mitchell, Finkelhor and Wolak, 2005; Wang *et al.*, 2005). Many of these parental actions speak of a generational divide in internet usage and knowledge, with the resultant effect of many parents even viewing their offspring as technological gurus, turning to them for answers, rather than the other way around. Relying solely on monitoring and filtering software, or on children's own good judgement and maturity, leaves a problem waiting to happen.

Research entitled 'Internet Parenting Styles and the Impact on Internet Use of Primary School Children' reports how much of a parental issue e-safety really is:

> Recent research – in developed countries – clearly indicates that internet use is mainly a home based activity. Up to 91.2 per cent of primary school children surf on the internet at home; in contrast to about 66 per cent at school. This introduces the critical role of parents in view of safe internet usage and internet education. (Valcke *et al.*, 2010, p.454)

Parenting styles can significantly alter children's use of technology – parents who have rules and boundaries for other behaviours in the home are more likely to monitor and limit their child's internet usage. Younger parents are also more likely to be aware of internet dangers and their children's behaviour, presumably because they are more au fait with technology and use it themselves. Permissive parenting styles will likely carry through to technology use, with children experiencing little or no supervision when using the internet and other tools. However, more aggressive parenting styles can lead to 'vigilante' style behaviour, fuelled by what Furedi describes as a 'culture of fear' (2006).

In a paper entitled *Everyday Fear: Parenting and Childhood in a Culture of Fear* Franklin suggests that in a society saturated by media, it is almost impossible to evade the latest focus of fear, and to avoid allowing these fears to drive our behaviours. She writes, 'with so much pressure on parents it is unsurprising that they do everything in their power to protect their children, even if it is from purely hypothetical risks, and unfortunately this can mean over-protection, over-supervision and overregulation' (Franklin and Cromby 2010, p.4).

As the media exploitation of parents' fears continues, with supposed constant dangers of paedophiles, predators and stranger danger on every corner, some parents can become almost unhealthily cautious of their children's online behaviour. Parents can struggle to know how to balance technology use. In the climate of fear we exist within in the Western world many parents feel it is essential, for example, for their child to have a mobile phone, yet simultaneously fear the dangers of cyber bullying, sexting and accessing inappropriate content that is proffered by the phone's gateway to the global world. Furedi states that the virtual world can encourage the fear of 'invisible strangers' to run riot in our imaginations (2002).

UK researchers at the University of Plymouth explored whether peer education is more effective to encourage safe online behaviour, rather than parental monitoring and restrictive processes that filter and block content. In a paper published by the Centre for Information Security and Network Research it was reported that 'many existing approaches to promoting internet awareness make use of the risk laden environment which can incite parents and carers to adopt an approach with excessive filtering and restrictive access. The more inclusive approach has focused on the empowerment of young people to promote internet awareness among their peers' (Atkinson, Furnell and Phippen 2009, p.1).

This may be important for schools to note – peer led education has been utilized for a variety of curriculum approaches, and e-safety may be a particularly good beneficiary of a peer-teaching, given the likelihood of young people understanding other students' online behaviours and tools far better than adults.

While it can seem like a logical approach for parents simply to reduce and monitor children's use of technology, this will largely fail to educate and build awareness in young people who may become more subversive in their use. There is the added danger that strict parental boundaries will only serve to discourage young people from turning to their parents for advice and support when they experience cyber bullying, or worse, inappropriate contact or sexting that gets out of hand. This is important to note for school staff – being someone to tell is crucial, particularly if young people don't feel able to discuss issues relating to e-safety with their parents.

Many parents and grandparents lack the knowledge and proficiency that seems to come naturally to children and young people, and will need some guidance to be able to initiate conversations, rules, and limits on their children's online behaviour. Providing basic tips and suggestions in a school newsletter or on the school website can be a good first step. For example:

- Keep desktop computers in a family room with the back of the screen against the wall, and insist that laptops are used only in comunal spaces to avoid children accessing inappropriate content away from adult eyes.

- Purchase filtering and monitoring software for your home computer. These easy to use tools are available online or from most electrical stores.

- Agree rules as a family about time spent online and technology use, and discuss what to do in an incident of cyber bullying, or when someone makes an online approach or inappropriate contact.

- Inform children of what to do when they receive files that are from people they don't know. It could be a virus, or inappropriate content not suitable for children's eyes.

- Google yourself regularly to check your privacy settings on social networking sites, and to check what other information is online about you.

- Check your privacy settings on social networking sites such as Facebook, so that only your friends or 'contacts' can see your information, status updates and photographs.

- Check what personal information you've posted online. Social networking profiles shouldn't contain any identifying information such as an address or date of birth.

- In the UK, report any issues of concern, including cyber bullying, to CEOP – the Child Exploitation and Online Protection centre, at www.CEOP.gov.uk. In the US, the National Cyber Security Alliance has a multi-purpose website to gain advice and support about online safety, www.staysafeonline.org, and the website www.stopbullying.gov provides advice about all types of bullying, including cyber.

- As parents, get informed – set up your own Facebook profile or Twitter account and understand the tools, for example.

It is for schools to decide whether they will support the e-safety education of parents, as well as students, and what form that might take. Proactive schools might host a parents' evening, perhaps during an anti-bullying awareness-raising session, exploring both e-safety and cyber bullying. A range of regional and national organizations provide posters and information leaflets that can be made available in the school entrance area.

Online Resources

There are a number of excellent websites that are good sources of information and resources for parents, professionals and young people.

UK Resources

- www.bbc.co.uk/schools/parents/cyber_bullying – information from the BBC to assist parents in understanding and managing their child's experiences of cyber bullying. Includes videos exploring the issue of cyber bullying.

- www.cybermentors.org.uk – a website for children and young people experiencing any form of bullying, including cyber, to gain information, advice and support from trained peer mentors and adult counsellors through an online chat platform, managed by the UK charity Beat Bullying.

- www.ceop.gov.uk – a website managed by the UK government, the Child Exploitation and Online Protection Centre (CEOP) works to eradicate the sexual abuse of children and young people, and publishes a number of resources to assist parents, professionals and young people to stay safe in the digital world. CEOP has developed the Safety Centre to encourage people to report online abuse and cyber bullying at www.ceop.police.uk/safety-centre.

- www.ThinkUKnow.co.uk – another CEOP site, ThinkUKnow provides a range of resources for children, young people, parents/carers and educators to introduce healthy and safe online behaviour. Resources include games, videos, lesson plans and school assemblies.

US Resources

- www.stopcyberbullying.org – information and advice about tackling cyber bullying, including definitions, school perspectives, the law as it relates to cyber bullying and a downloadable Stop Cyber Bullying Toolkit for schools and young people.

- www.netsmartz.org – a website from the National Center for Missing and Exploited Children, NetSmartz provides age-appropriate resources to help teach children and young people aged 5–17 how to be safer online and offline. Resources include videos, games, activity cards and presentations for parents, educators and law enforcement.

- www.cyber-safety.com – a website dedicated to helping children stay safe online. Provides safety tips, news and downloadable materials about cyber bullying and e-safety.

Chapter 6

Cyber Bullying

Cyber bullying is an issue closely associated with e-safety, and is arguably the most common problem experienced by young people when using technology. Hinduja and Patchin define cyber bullying as the 'willful and repeated harm inflicted through the use of computers, cell phones, and other electronic devices' (2009, p.5). Belsey (2004) defined cyber bullying as a phenomenon that '…involves the use of information and communication technologies to support deliberate, repeated, and hostile behavior by an individual or group that is intended to harm others' (p.1).

The issue of cyber bullying is only as old as the technologies used to hurt and denigrate others, and as such, the research and study of cyber bullying is still growing, but perhaps not as fast as the phenomenon itself. It stands to reason that any technology can be used for both positive and negative effect, but the extremes to which mobile phones, online platforms and other forms of technology are abused to bully others often leaves parents, youths and teachers astounded. 'Traditional' forms of bullying, a term used to denote those incidents which typically take place in the school yard or classroom, were difficult enough to identify and punish. The advent of cyber bullying can elevate both the cruelty and severity of the attacks, and cyber bullying is often without a clear initiator, due to the anonymity afforded by the medium and the crowd-effect of the bullying.

There are seven types of cyber bullying:

1. *Flaming*: sending angry, rude, vulgar messages directed at a person or persons privately or to an online group.

2. *Harassment*: repeatedly sending a person offensive messages.

3. *Denigration*: sending/posting rumours, harmful, untrue information about the person to others.

4. *Cyberstalking*: harassment that includes threats of harm or is highly intimidating.

5. *Impersonation or masquerading*: pretending to be another person and posting/sending material online to make them look bad.

6. *Outing or trickery*: tricking a person into sending information (secrets, embarrassing information) that can be used to send to others online.

7. *Exclusion*: excluding someone purposefully from an online group (IM list).

(Willard, 2007)

A variety of technological tools and platforms are used to conduct these forms of bullying, including text message or phone call; videoing or taking pictures of someone with a digital camera, or more commonly a mobile phone; using email; bullying in chat rooms or using instant messaging (IM); and via social networking sites, such as writing an abusive status update on someone's Facebook profile. As the technology grows and changes, so too will the methods used to cyber bully.

A number of research studies have been conducted to identify the prevalence of cyber bullying, with some reports suggesting that it is a problem of epidemic proportions, while others find cyber bullying to be on par in frequency with other forms. A recent study conducted by Anglia Ruskin University, commissioned by the National Children's Bureau, found that nearly one in five (18.4%) of UK youngsters have been victims of cyber bullying, with girls affected more than boys, but two thirds (66%) of those questioned said they had witnessed cyber bullying or known someone who has been a victim – seemingly a disparate number reporting that it had occurred to 'someone else'. The study also reported that less than half (45%) said they would look for support if they experienced cyber bullying (O'Brien and Moules, 2010).

In the USA, the Indicators of School Crime and Safety survey found that 7,066,000 US students ages 12 to 18 reported they were bullied at school within the academic year, equivalent to 28 per cent, with 1,521,000 or 6 per cent reporting they experienced cyber bullying both on or off school property (Robers, Zhang and Truman, 2012).

Like the tools used to perpetrate cyber bullying, the *issue* of cyber bullying is complex. Young people have suggested that cyber bullying is one of the main challenges they face in the digital world (Cross *et al.*, 2009). In a paper published by the University of Calgary, researchers explored the problems often compounding cyber bullying. They write:

> according to Willard (2006), there are three related concerns in addition to the seven types of cyber bullying. These concerns include the disclosure of massive amounts of personal information via the internet by students, how students become addicted to the internet to the point where their lives are highly dependent on the time they spend online, and the prevalence of suicide and self-harm communities in which youth that are depressed will access to obtain information on suicide and self-harm methods. (Li and Lambert 2010, p.4)

The 24/7 nature of the technology young people use, and the almost constant state of connection and communication, suggests what a problem cyber bullying can be, not only for the victim, but their peers, family, onlookers or bystanders, and school, as well as the bully themselves. In the case of cyber bullying via the internet or mobile phones, a reluctance to disengage from technology and the desire to be privy to what others are saying can keep victims and bystanders locked to their screens – a terrible voyeuristic cycle of watching bullying play out and feeling powerless to take action, or worse, the continual re-experience of the bullying as victims re-read and live their torment through the preserved words on their computer screen or mobile phone.

Given the often very public platform through which cyber bullying takes place, for example on a social networking site, the likelihood is that a wide audience will not only see the bullying but be compelled to contribute. The so-called 'bystander effect' can encourage others to unwittingly join in with the bully, whom they may believe to be joking or messing around. The difficulty of reading emotion and intent in online statements can create a sense of ambiguity about whether an aggressor is bullying or 'just kidding' which may encourage others to contribute. The lack of non-verbal cues not only leaves the bystanders unclear about whether bullying is taking place or not, but can also leave the victim in a similar state. A young person may not realize they are being bullied because of a later retraction of the intent, 'I was only joking', or worse, may feel quite sure they are experiencing cyber bullying but not be able to prove their aggressor's intent.

Additionally, the distancing effect of cyber bullying serves to remove the naturally occurring empathic emotional response that will usually be elicited in those witnessing school yard or traditional bullying. Seeing a person's pain, unease, discomfort or terror can leave no doubt as to the effects of the bully's actions, and will hopefully stir at least some students to help. Those witnessing this awful act play out will know quite clearly the impact of their own actions if they choose to join in, but this is often not the case when using technology. The ease with which a supporting comment is made of the bully's actions on a social networking site, for example, coupled with the lack of visual emotional feedback from the victim, can leave bystanders completely unaware of their actions. Similarly, forwarding on a picture or video of a person being bullied takes little more than a click. Young people can defend their innocence with ignorance; after all, they were not the one who took the image, nor who forwarded it onwards in the first place. This bystander culpability is something that needs to be taught in our schools and homes if cyber bullying is to be effectively tackled.

The bystander effect also speaks of the potentially vast numbers of people who will see a cyber bullying incident take place if a 'viral' spreading of a comment, image or video takes place. The relatively new phenomenon of something going viral describes the way in which the internet can be used to spread a bullying act to thousands, or even millions of people. High profile cases of young people taking their own lives after encountering such a spreading of their humiliation are a clear indicator of the potential danger of cyber bullying. Not only is the degradation witnessed by those in the classroom, or worse their online social network, but by strangers all over the world. The potential for depression, anxiety, social isolation, or worse, suicide, is great when a person's most intimately painful moments are broadcast for all to see.

Girls Versus Boys

There is a difference in opinion between researchers as to whether cyber bullying is a phenomenon that is perpetrated by and affects more girls than boys. With both sexes using the technology it is arguable that both experience cyber bullying, and could be just as likely to commit it. Certainly, more young people are reported to be cyber than traditional bullies, perhaps in part due to the bystander effect. Researchers report that the anonymity of some forms of cyber bullying encourages people to say and do things they would be unlikely to directly. This inhibition increases not only the number of potential perpetrators of cyber bullying but also the magnitude of threats, taunts, and so on, that they are willing to deliver (Kowalski, Limber and Agatston, 2008).

Lenhart (2007) and Smith *et al.* (2008) claim that girls are more likely to be involved in cyber bullying, perhaps due to the increased likelihood of girls utilizing relationally aggressive tactics which can be suitably employed online, such as isolation, rumour and gossip spreading, and otherwise damaging and manipulating relationships to gain power and control. Hinduja and Patchin (2009) found that girls engaged in cyber bullying for longer than boys, and employed different tactics, including secretly taking pictures of victims and posting them online.

A School Issue

This all paints a worrying picture for schools. The very nature of cyber bullying, the potential damage it can do and the grey line between incidents being a school or home issue often leave many educators confused, wary of becoming involved, or encountering a deluge of difficult to solve cases. As has been mentioned before, schools have a legal duty of care towards students, and have a responsibility to tackle all forms of bullying, but confusion occurs when many incidents of cyber bullying take place outside of the school grounds and school time. Many schools ban students from using mobile phones, and most school-owned technology employs the necessary filtering software to – it is hoped – prevent cyber bullying from taking place. However, it would be naïve of us to believe that incidents of bullying using technology don't take place during the school day, and that issues that occur at home don't affect young people during school time.

Any student on the receiving end of vicious and humiliating cyber bullying will either be too fearful or embarrassed to return to school, thus missing academic time, or be too emotionally distraught to effectively learn. This then, naturally, becomes a school issue as we have seen.

Educators should therefore consider their role carefully: failure to act upon incidents of cyber bullying that occurred during school time or that effect a students' ability to learn constitutes a failure of care, and contradicts the school anti-bullying policy. In an increasingly litigious society, schools need to not only protect students, but also themselves as an institution. The 'Preventing and Tackling Bullying' guidance produced by the Department for Education in the UK states:

> Head teachers have a specific statutory power to discipline students for poor behaviour outside of the school premises. Section 89(5) of the Education and Inspections Act 2006 gives head teachers the power to regulate students' conduct when they are not on school premises and are not under the lawful control or charge of a member of school staff (*this legislation does not apply to independent schools*). This can relate to any bullying incidents occurring anywhere off the school premises, such as on school or public transport, outside the local shops, or in a town or village centre. (2012, p.4)

As a starting point it is advisable to review your school anti-bullying policy, and ensure that it contains a reference to cyber bullying, including a definition and an outline of how cyber bullying might occur, and clearly state what the school intends to do if an incident is reported. At the very least the policy should make reference to the inclusion of cyber bullying as a theme within the curriculum, perhaps during ICT lessons, in order to educate students to prevent incidents from occurring in the future. The lesson plans provided at the back of this book include cyber bullying and can be used within the curriculum.

Your policy should indicate when parents will be informed and involved, as with any bullying incident, and should clearly state that any incidents deemed serious enough or which may be a criminal offence will be reported to the police. It is worth noting that some forms of cyber bullying are indeed criminal offences, such as cyber stalking and harassment, and thus are punishable by law. In the UK the Protection from Harassment Act 1997, the Malicious Communications Act 1988, the Communications Act 2003 and the Public Order Act 1986 can all relate to forms of cyber bullying, while in the USA laws can vary by state. Most US states have bullying laws, whereby acts of bullying can be deemed criminal offences; however, few include or reference cyber bullying specifically. When cyber bullying involves threats of violence, child pornography or sending sexually explicit messages or photos, stalking, hate crimes or an invasion of privacy, it is considered a crime. Additionally, the Megan Meier Cyberbullying Prevention Act (2009) states that 'whoever transmits in interstate or foreign commerce any communication, with the intent to coerce, intimidate, harass, or cause substantial emotional distress to a person, using electronic means to support severe, repeated, and hostile behavior, shall be fined under this title or imprisoned not more than two years, or both' (United States Code, 2009, sec 3:881).

In the UK government guidance produced by the Department for Education notes that schools have powers with regard to tackling cyber bullying. 'The wider search powers included in the Education Act 2011 give teachers stronger powers to tackle cyber-bullying by providing a specific power to search for and, if necessary, delete inappropriate images (or files) on electronic devices, including mobile phones' (2012, p.4). Schools should ensure that any intent to search students, and particularly access content on mobile phones or other devices, is clearly detailed in the school behaviour policy, and any such search is conducted with at least two members of staff present.

Dealing with individual incidents of cyber bullying can be a minefield for staff, as they seek to unravel the complicated web of 'who did what to whom'. Educating students to understand what constitutes cyber bullying, the role of the bystander and the impact of cyber bullying is crucial, and will serve to prevent such incidents from occurring in the future. Utilizing school counselling services and outside agencies to deliver cyber bullying awareness sessions can help victims and perpetrators to receive the support they need, and reinforce the message of the unacceptability of cyber bullying in your school.

It is important to note that cyber bullying can affect staff, as well as students. Teaching and support staff are just as much at risk of becoming a target for cyber harassment, bashing and denigration as young people, and as such, policies and procedures should ensure every member of the school community is supported. A 2009 survey conducted by the Teacher Support Network and The Association of Teachers and Lecturers reported that 15 per cent of teachers had been victims of cyber bullying (ATL, 2009). The largest teaching union in the UK, NASUWT, surveyed teachers over a period of 5 days on cyber bullying, with almost 100 teachers reporting real distress and trauma caused by incidents of cyber bullying by students using mobile phones and web-based sites (NASUWT, 2012).

Educating staff about how to stay safe from cyber bullying is as important as educating students: staff should never give personal phone numbers, email addresses or other contact information to students, and any staff members using a social networking site should be mindful to check their privacy settings and avoid adding students or ex-students to their contacts or 'friends' lists. Many students may wish to befriend a teacher on Facebook or Twitter, for example, usually with positive intentions. However, this can muddy the waters of appropriate teacher–student relationships and also put other staff at risk of cyber bullying or harassment. Consider the impact of photographs of the staff Christmas party uploaded on a Facebook page by a member of staff who is 'friends' with a student from school. The student has access to the pictures which can be easily downloaded, copied and shared, without the consent of the teacher in question, and certainly without the knowledge of any other people posing in the images who may not even be aware their photographs have been displayed on Facebook for all to see.

Your teaching and support staff may have little understanding about the impact of their online behaviour, and while it is inappropriate for schools to dictate how people communicate and interact online, highlighting the dangers and potential problems can help everyone stay informed and become aware.

As an age-old problem, bullying is unlikely ever to be eradicated from our schools and communities, but we each play a role in trying to reach that goal nevertheless. Staff training, the circulation of policy and procedures, the inclusion of cyber bullying in the curriculum and a clear communication of zero tolerance for bullying will all seek to ensure your school is better equipped and prepared to prevent and effectively respond to incidents as they occur.

Chapter 7

E-Safety as a Whole School Issue

As with any issue that can potentially affect the whole school community, it is advisable that a school-wide approach is taken to the teaching, promotion and monitoring of e-safety, not only with students, but also with staff, governors or school board members, and parents and carers. Simply slotting e-safety into an area of the curriculum may go some way to developing students' understanding, but will do little to educate staff, raise awareness with parents of how to keep their children safe at home, and monitor staff and students' uses of school technology. Given the potential seriousness of a misuse or abuse of technology there is a clear need for a coordinated and consistent message about e-safety across the school, embedding e-safety into the curriculum, into the daily usage of technology by students and staff, and into the policies and procedures already in place in school.

Adopting a Whole School Approach

Developing a school-wide policy is a first step to creating a consistent and shared understanding of e-safety which can then be effectively communicated to all members of the school community through appropriate methods and channels. A policy should summarize the stance of the school in their response and reaction to e-safety and should underpin the core messages about technology that are evident throughout the school. The policy, as a working document, forms the basis for how e-safety will be addressed, promoted, taught and monitored, and is a source of reference for staff, governors or school boards, and parents and carers, and should be made available or communicated in an appropriate way to students.

Creating a school response to e-safety will clearly be an ongoing process and cannot be the work of solely one person. For any policy or practice to be adopted by the whole, there is a need for buy-in and understanding across the school, and a shared sense of ownership and cooperation, ensuring that the responsibility to communicate and practise e-safety is both individual and shared.

With an over-arching policy in place as a strategic plan and documentation of the school vision and stance on e-safety, the role of individuals is then to promote and deliver the policy and act in accordance with its contents.

The following table indicates the general roles of staff, governors or school boards, students, and parents and carers.

Staff	Governors or School Boards	Students	Parents and Carers
Roles To read and follow the policy To ensure staff use of school technologies is appropriate and agreed To ensure that staff use of private technologies (e.g. private mobile phones) is appropriate and in accordance with the policy To ensure that messages of e-safety are taught and communicated effectively and appropriately to students when using any information communication technology (ICT) equipment To act in accordance with the policy when misuses or abuse of technology are witnessed or reported To invoke child protection procedures if necessary	**Roles** To contribute to the creation of the policy To assist in ensuring the policy is effectively communicated and promoted to all members of the school community To effectively monitor and evaluate the effectiveness of the policy To hear any complaints of technology misuse or abuse against or by students or staff that are deemed serious or when raised as a formal complaint To review the policy annually or when deemed necessary, e.g. when new technology is introduced to the school	**Roles** To read and follow the policy To act in accordance with the policy when using any school ICT equipment To develop an awareness and understanding of e-safety via curriculum delivery To be involved in the creation and monitoring of the e-safety policy when necessary (e.g. school council) To assist in the promotion of key e-safety messages and communicating these messages to other students (e.g. member of the school council developing literature for others) To report any misuse or abuse of technology that they are victim to, party to or witnessing to a member of staff	**Roles** To read and follow the policy To communicate the core messages of the policy and key aspects of e-safety to their children when using technology outside of school To support the school in delivering an e-safety curriculum To be aware of the technologies deemed appropriate to be brought into school To report any misuse or abuse of technology that their child is victim to, party to or witnessing to a member of staff

Figure 7.1 A school-wide policy on e-safety

Generating a Whole-school Response to E-Safety: School Responsibilities

While an e-safety policy forms the bedrock of a school-wide response to the issue, an effective whole-school approach is multi-faceted and ensures the policy is implemented, cutting across all strands of school planning and organization, including the curriculum, staff training and awareness raising, behaviour, discipline and sanctions, and engaging the wider members of the school community, such as school governors or school board members, and parents and carers.

The following highlights the different aspects of implementation that should ideally be considered to create an effective whole-school response to e-safety.

E-Safety and the School Improvement Plan

If a school is aiming to fully consider and evaluate an effective response to the issue of e-safety, it is highly advisable to consider including e-safety in the School Improvement Plan, highlighting concrete actions and timelines for implementation. This will ensure that the issue is considered at the highest school level by the head teacher and senior leadership team (SLT), and gain support and assistance from local advisors, agencies and other relevant teams and professionals, who should be able to assist on staff training, curriculum development and more.

Appointing an E-Safety Coordinator

To ensure that an effective and considered response to e-safety is achieved, particularly if outlined in the School Improvement Plan, it is advisable to appoint a member of staff with responsibility for coordinating e-safety in school. This is also advisable, given that it is highly likely that once awareness is raised and students begin to be educated on the risks and dangers, as well as responsibilities, of using technology, there will potentially be an increase in the number of reports of the misuse or abuse of technology. This includes the possibility that some children will feel encouraged to report serious complaints, including those of a child protection nature; for example, being the victim of an assault or sexual harassment after meeting someone online.

The E-safety Coordinator should therefore be a member of staff with a proven record and ability to perform in a pastoral role: he or she will need to support individual children and parents, as well as oversee the implementation of the policy and specific pieces of work, such as the development of an e-safety curriculum, linking with the ICT coordinators and other pastoral staff. This member of staff will need to be supported by the Senior Leadership Team and be aware of who is the school Child Protection Coordinator and Special Educational Needs Coordinator.

The E-Safety Coordinator will ensure that the policy is effectively monitored and reviewed annually, and will coordinate the implementation of specific strands or pieces of work, such as raising awareness with parents and carers or developing a staff code of conduct.

Developing a Whole-school Policy

As previously discussed, an e-safety policy is essential for the effective and coordinated roll-out of e-safety work across the school, but is only as good as its implementation. An excellent policy that isn't distributed, monitored or reviewed is useless.

For schools appointing an E-Safety Coordinator, an integral part of their role should be to develop the policy, in conjunction with all members of the school community.

Staff Code of Conduct

Ensuring that students are using technology safely is only one piece of the puzzle. Staff are just as likely to be the targets of an abuse of technology, or to misuse it (either knowingly or ignorantly).

Incidents of staff becoming the victim of cyber bullying, or adding students as contacts on social networking sites are becoming increasingly common. A Staff Code of Conduct should outline their responsibilities for using ICT in school and can explore how to protect staff from inappropriate behaviour outside of the school gates. A sample Staff Code of Conduct can be found in the appendices.

Student Code of Conduct

Similarly, a Student Code of Conduct, to be signed by the student and a parent or carer, should outline how students are expected to use ICT in school, and the school's stance on abuses of technology outside of school. Schools may also want to consider creating an e-safety rules consent form for students to sign and refer to, or creating e-safety rules to be displayed near each computer in school and in ICT suites. Ensuring that parents and carers sign the Code of Conduct will assist with raising awareness of the issue and gaining their support in tackling the problem of abuse and misuse of technology.

Updating the School Behaviour Policy

To reflect the new school rules relating to the use of technology, it is important to ensure the school behaviour policy is updated to reflect the changes, coordinating the sanctions cited for the misuse or abuse of technology and other incidents of poor behaviour. It is also important to consider cyber bullying within the school anti-bullying policy, coordinating with and referring to the e-safety policy, stating how incidents will be dealt with and how to report cyber bullying.

Raising Awareness with Parents and Carers

As previously mentioned, it is imperative that parents and carers have an understanding of the importance of e-safety and how to protect their children at home, given that most misuses of technology will occur outside of the school gates where technology isn't monitored or filtered. Many parents will have a limited knowledge in comparison to their children, and providing a simple overview of what e-safety is and how to protect and educate children in the home will help to reduce incidents from occurring.

Raising Awareness in School

As well as engaging in continual and appropriate awareness-raising and education with students, it is advisable to place a concerted emphasis on e-safety at specific times, such as during National Anti-Bullying Week or Bullying Prevention Month, and on Safer Internet Day.

Exploring the Role of Staff

While educating students is crucial, it is also imperative that all staff have an awareness of e-safety and understand how the technology can be misused within their own curriculum areas, classrooms and across the school as a whole. Staff should be aware of the school's policies and practices when using ICT as a teaching tool, research or planning aid, and as such any e-safety policy should contain clear and appropriate guidelines for staff, as well as students, to adhere to. Staff also need to be aware of what is acceptable in terms of their own use of school technology and use of personal technology while working, e.g. accessing private email in school and the consequences of accessing inappropriate or unsuitable materials in school via school or private equipment, and engaging in illegal or inappropriate conduct through the use of technology.

Conversely, there have been many incidents of staff being the victim of students' abuse of technology, and complaints procedures and support mechanisms for adults are necessary in conjunction with clear sanctions and disciplinary procedures for students.

While e-safety is a whole school issue, there are differing roles and levels of engagement for staff to assist in the development of a school-wide approach. Class teachers and subject leaders may only need to be aware of the e-safety policy and consider the implications of e-safety within their own subject areas or when a lesson utilizes ICT as a teaching and learning tool, in addition to generally ensuring that students are made aware of the school policies and procedures, such as communicating the message that the use of mobile phones in school is prohibited.

Subject Leaders for ICT and PSHE

Subject leaders for ICT, Personal Social Health Education (PSHE), school counsellors or those responsible for student well-being will play a more definitive role in teaching and communicating e-safety messages to students. Ensuring that e-safety is included in the ICT curriculum for all students is imperative, supported by the inclusion of topics such as cyber bullying within the PSE curriculum that link to the core messages of e-safety. Opportunities to reinforce messages of e-safety should not be overlooked, and engagement in activities such as presentations, assemblies, workshops and projects within Anti-Bullying Week or for Safer Internet Day are extremely useful.

Engaging school council members and peer supporters or buddies is also a useful way to promote e-safety and can be an effective method to communicate core messages to students, using the voice of their peers which may be more likely to be heard.

Pastoral Teams and Senior Leadership Teams

Pastoral teams and senior leadership teams should consider the implications of responding to the welfare of students when there is an incident of ICT misuse or abuse, and the legislative framework when considering e-safety. Some instances of technology misuse will be criminal offences that a student (or member of staff) may perpetrate or be a victim of. There is also the implication of potential child protection protocols and policies being influenced by promoting e-safety, and pastoral staff should have a clear understanding of when a misuse or abuse of technology could indicate a potential child protection investigation, and the appropriate course of action to be followed, in accordance with the school child protection policy.

It is also the role of pastoral teams to ensure that students affected by breaches of e-safety have access to appropriate support either in school or via external agencies, particularly in serious incidents where a child may have been victim to physical or sexual abuse. It is also worth considering how to encourage students to report incidents to staff, including through peer supporters such as peer listeners or buddies or more private methods such as via a school email address. Peer support schemes can be extremely effective in allowing students to have access to immediate emotional support and listening, and many young people report feeling more confident to discuss worries or concerns with peers. However, ensuring that students acting in a supportive role have adequate and appropriate training and support from staff is crucial. If a school is promoting to students the messages of e-safety and encouraging access to peer supporters for advice and information, should they be concerned, then peer supporters need to be equipped with a clear understanding of what e-safety is, how to stay safe online, what cyber bullying is and how to manage it, and most important should have clear and direct access to staff, ideally pastoral staff, to report anything of concern raised by a student and to refer on those who cannot be helped by a peer supporter.

All staff who witness an incident of misuse or abuse of technology or to whom an incident is reported should know the correct procedure and protocols for recording and monitoring the incident, and the appropriate sanctions and course of action to be taken, linked to the school behaviour management policy. This should all be outlined within the school e-safety policy.

Head Teacher

The head teacher holds the overall responsibility for e-safety and maintaining a safe ICT environment, and as such should coordinate, develop and promote effective policies to support staff in the awareness, development and delivery of e-safety. The head teacher should also act as the link to the school governing body or school board to ensure that they are informed and consulted on policy and curriculum changes and developments.

The head teacher, senior leadership team or a network manager (should a school have one) are also responsible for maintaining ICT equipment, including its safe and responsible use by staff, ensuring that appropriate monitoring and filtering equipment is in place on school computers and there are clear procedures to respond to the discovery of inappropriate use or content found on school equipment.

The Role of Students

Given that young people are so adept and proficient at using the technology, there is a clear role for students to be involved in the creation and dissemination of e-safety messages. The potential discrepancies between staff and student use of technology may mean that staff have less knowledge and awareness of the aspects of the technology that they wish to educate students on; for example, educating students on the safe and responsible use of social networking sites. Therefore, peer led education may be an extremely useful and effective way to promote e-safety, particularly as messages from peers may be more likely to be heard and understood by young people, as they recognize that the deliverer has an understanding of the importance of technology and uses it in a similar fashion. There is a danger that some students will be less likely to engage in e-safety education delivered by teachers whom they perceive not to understand the technology or to have vastly differing uses to them. There is of course the fact that some staff members will have a poor or limited understanding of technology and may struggle to teach or respond to e-safety, highlighting the importance of staff training and support.

School council members or peer supporters, such as trained buddies, peer listeners or peer mediators, generally hold a responsible and recognized role within the school, and are well placed to deliver structured lessons and presentations to their peers. Working with a member of staff, these students can develop, design and deliver lessons throughout the school, as well as assemblies and workshops. They may even be willing to design and produce information to students such as leaflets, posters and information for student planners. These students are also well-placed to communicate messages of reporting incidents of technology misuse or abuse and promoting the various methods available to students to do this, including through the technology itself. For example, you can now report incidents of cyber bullying, sexual abuse, harmful online content and more directly to the UK Child Exploitation and Online Protection centre (CEOP) at www.ceop.gov.uk.

The Role of Parents and Carers

Involving parents and carers in any school venture or the promotion of an issue of concern is key to ensuring a consistent message is delivered at home as well as in school. With e-safety this is particularly relevant as the protection offered by school computers, such as filtering and monitoring software, is often absent from home computers, and with many children now owning mobile devices with wireless internet access there is the likelihood that they will come into contact with harmful or inappropriate content outside of the school gates.

Many parents, like most adults, do not use the technology in the same way as children and young people, and may lack an understanding of what it is their children use the technology for and how it works, making it difficult to know how to protect them from potential dangers or harm and how to instil an understanding of personal responsibility and safety.

Included in the appendices is a parent and carer questionnaire that will allow a school to gain the views and perceptions of parents about both their use of technology and their children's use. Used in conjunction with the student questionnaire, also found in the appendices, the results will indicate how parents and students' use of technology may differ and the potentially divergent perceptions of what parents may think of their children's uses of technology and their children's responses. Results of the questionnaires will allow schools to develop more effective e-safety schemes of work, monitor any improvements in safe and responsible behaviour if the questionnaires are periodically repeated, and indicate where and how to target other resources, such as providing awareness-raising presentations to parents, for example.

Chapter 8

Creating an E-Safety Policy

Central to the creation of a whole-school approach to e-safety is an e-safety policy. Many schools may already have an internet policy, or an acceptable use policy, which goes some way to begin to outline the school's stance on the use of technology, in particular students' use of the internet. However, e-safety encompasses a far wider remit than just the internet, including various other technologies such as mobile phones and wireless communication devices, and an e-safety policy should explore not only how to minimize risks and manage students' behaviour, but also that of staff, and highlight the important role of parents and carers in promoting e-safety in the home. An e-safety policy should also highlight proactive or preventative measures to promote and develop awareness of e-safety across the school, in addition to outlining how and when to react to incidents of misuse or abuse of technology, with clear links to other school policies such as the child protection policy, anti-bullying policy and behaviour management policy.

It is advised that an e-safety policy encompass any similar policies, such as acceptable use policies, to avoid duplication of information and ensure that a consistent and coordinated message is presented throughout the school.

Overview of Policy Contents

It is important that an e-safety policy is created to meet the needs of a school, and as such is considered and developed with the school in mind. Using model or template policies is a good starting point to ensure that the most salient points are included; however, given the diverse and differing nature of schools, the technology available in schools and students' usage of technology, it is advisable the policy is individualized.

Consider:

- How do students use technology in this school, as a part of the curriculum, as a learning and teaching tool and for personal use?

- Have there been any recent incidents of misuse of technology?

- Are incidents of misuse or abuse of technology occurring outside of school becoming a school issue?

- Do staff have a full understanding and awareness of e-safety in this school?

- Who monitors the technology used in this school, including updating filtering software?

- Who in this school can take a lead on e-safety?

- Who needs to be involved in creating the e-safety policy?

- Do parents and carers have a full understanding of e-safety?

- Do staff currently know how to respond to an incident of misuse or abuse of technology in or outside of school?

- Where is the greatest need, in terms of initiating e-safety education, awareness-raising or support?

- Are staff currently protected from being potential targets of an abuse or misuse of technology by students?

- Are staff aware of their Code of Conduct for using ICT in school, and when communicating with students or parents outside of school?

An e-safety policy should include:

- **A definition of e-safety**
  A definition that is easily understandable, clear, concise and without technological jargon; for example, not using IM to mean instant messaging without explanation.

- **Purpose of policy**
  A statement to outline why an e-safety policy has been created and what will be included.

- **Why e-safety is important/the impact of technology across the school**
  A statement exploring the importance of e-safety and how it affects students, staff, and parents and carers. This can be linked to the potential dangers and risks associated with the use of technology by children.

- **The utilization of ICT in school**
  Exploring how and why technology is used throughout the school, and for what purpose. This should begin to make clear that technology is provided in school for a specific purpose, that is, to enhance teaching and learning, and as such there are expectations for all members of the school community to conform to the school's rules when using ICT. It may also be of benefit in this section to explore how young people may use technology outside of school, and the differences in use thereof.

- **Reference to other policies**
  An e-safety policy should reference and relate to other school policies, including the child protection policy, anti-bullying policy and behaviour management policy. It is important to ensure that the contents of the policies are consistent; for example, sanctions and discipline procedures for the misuse of technology or cyber bullying are consistent with the sanctions invoked for similar examples of poor behaviour.

- **Teaching and learning**
  This section should outline why and how e-safety will be taught to students, including who will coordinate schemes of work for teaching e-safety and the relation between the teaching of e-safety and similar topics in other areas of the curriculum, e.g. exploring cyber bullying within the Personal Social Health Education (PSHE) curriculum. The policy should

also outline the additional methods utilized to promote e-safety across the school, such as assemblies, workshops, use of external agencies and the promotion of e-safe behaviour and school rules for using technology by all members of staff when appropriate.

- **Managing internet access**

  Schools must decide on the appropriate balance between controlling and monitoring access to the technologies and setting rules for use, with educating students to be safe and responsible. As previously discussed, simply blocking or filtering all unwanted content from the internet and banning mobile phones in school may minimize the risk of incidents, but will do little to protect children at home or when using mobile wireless devices. This section should also include the school rules for gaining internet access for specific activities, such as private email and accessing social networking sites, as well as issues such as publishing images on the web and the appropriate use of the school website or email system, for both staff and students.

- **Managing additional technologies**

  As with the section above, the e-safety policy should also include information relating to how other technologies should be managed or used in school, such as school technological equipment, for example, digital cameras, Smart Boards, video cameras, mobile phones and private equipment, such as staff personal mobile phones and cameras. This section should clearly outline what is authorized to be used in school and what isn't, for staff and students.

- **Cyber bullying**

  Given that the majority of incidents of misuse or abuses of technology being dealt with by schools will be of a bullying nature, it is advisable to include a separate, specific section on cyber bullying in the e-safety policy that is consistent with or duplicated in the anti-bullying policy. This should define cyber bullying, outline the school's stance on reporting and investigating incidents of cyber bullying, and how it will be proactively tackled for example, linking to e-safety and PSHE. Consideration should also be given to the possibility that staff may be the victim of cyber bullying.

- **Authorizing access**

  This section should provide details of the Staff Code of Conduct, Student Code of Conduct and parent/carer agreement for the use of technologies in school.

- **Responding to incidents of e-safety**

  This section should outline how students, parents and staff can report incidents or complaints of unsafe, abusive or bullying behaviour via technology, including to whom they can report. Consideration should be given to additional methods for students to report, for those who do not feel confident in approaching a member of staff, for example, to peer listeners. This section should also include information about how incidents will be investigated and recorded and provide specific advice for staff to follow, ensuring consistency across the school. Links should also be made with child protection procedures, should an issue of e-safety become a child protection concern.

- **Staff roles and responsibilities**

  The responsibilities of all staff should be clearly outlined, including the responsibility of staff not to misuse technologies, linked to the Staff Code of Conduct. All staff members should be aware of their professional responsibilities when using ICT to communicate with and teach students. This section should also include any details of staff training provided to explore e-safety and/or introduce the policy.

- **Introducing the policy**

  This section should outline how the policy will be introduced across the school and the allocated timeframe for doing so. You may wish to consider creating student and parent-friendly versions containing the most salient points.

- **Monitoring, evaluation and review**

  The policy should reference when and how it will be monitored for its effectiveness, and by whom, and provide a date for review – an annual review is advisable, given the changing and developing nature of the technologies.

Writing an E-Safety Policy

Creating a whole-school response to e-safety undoubtedly requires a whole-school effort, and the writing of an e-safety policy should not be within one person's remit, given the complexity of the subject and the potential seriousness of a young person being the victim or perpetrator of a misuse or abuse of technology. One person's perspective will undoubtedly be too limited to gain an over-arching view on what e-safety issues are present within the school or need to be addressed.

Creating a Working Group

Creating a school working group to write and develop an effective policy and response to e-safety is an ideal starting point to gain the expertise and experience of various members of staff, both within and external to the school. The working group could contain:

- head teacher or member of the senior leadership team

- a member of pastoral staff

- ICT curriculum leader and/or PSHE curriculum leader or staff responsible for well-being

- a governor or school board representative

- a parent representative

- a student representative (e.g. member of the school council)

- ICT network coordinator or systems manager.

Your local education authority or school district may also have relevant and experienced professionals who can assist you in the development and dissemination of e-safety, including ICT advisory staff, anti-bullying specialists, or in some areas, e-safety specialists.

Gaining the Views of Students

Given the generally divergent uses of technology by young people and adults, it is important to gain the views and experiences of students about how they use technology, for what purpose and their experiences of misuse or abuse of the technology. Consulting with school council members is a useful place to start, or engage the school council in conducting more intensive research across the school by facilitating a student questionnaire. A student questionnaire is an extremely useful tool to ascertain what the potential e-safety issues may be within your school to allow the creation of a specific and targeted response to e-safety. A sample student questionnaire can be found in the appendices.

Gaining the views of Parents and Carers

As previously discussed, in addition to seeking the views and experiences of students, it may also be useful to explore parents' and carers' understanding of e-safety and uses of technology. Inviting a parent representative to sit on a policy working group could highlight the needs of parents and provide feedback as to how they may need to be supported or educated in e-safety to better support their children at home. Conducting a parent and carer questionnaire may also be useful to gain an insight into how children use technology at home to inform the e-safety curriculum and target work in school.

Chapter 9

Responding to Incidents

Responding to incidents of technology abuse and misuse can be complex and time consuming. It is important that incidents are fully investigated, as any other incident of poor behaviour would be, and given the potentially sensitive nature of incidents of technology misuse and abuse it is advisable to have a clear and consistent strategy for reporting, investigating, recording and monitoring that is communicated to all staff. Many schools benefit from appointing a lead member of staff to coordinate this process and to develop e-safety work as a whole, including within the curriculum, to ensure consistency. In this case all other staff, including auxiliary members, should know to refer any incident of cyber bullying or e-safety concern to this staff person.

Students should know they can report an issue of concern to any member of staff, though it is likely that young people will choose to confide in the person they view as most approachable or with whom they have the closest relationship. In this case, it may not be a senior member of staff or even a teacher to whom an incident is first reported. The school caretaker or custodian, nurse, librarian or lunchtime supervisor might be the first to hear. It is important, therefore, that all staff members are aware of the policy and procedures.

Creating a 'telling culture' is a feat in itself, and takes time. Young people are often wary of disclosing information to adults that might label them a telltale or 'grass', or worse, lead them to become the victim themselves next time. Such is the fear of repercussion, young people often fail to report at all, and similarly students may fear punishment themselves, such is the nature of incidents of risky behaviour online, even if they are not the victim. A young woman who meets a supposed boy online and is the eventual victim of an act of grooming by an adult male can feel as though she will be as much or more to blame in her parents' or schools' eyes, often compounded by the words and messages she receives from her attacker in a bid to keep her silent. Such is the shame, embarrassment and fear, many young people will keep private the horrific experiences perpetrated against them, and with it their depression, guilt and terror. As caring adults we must be open and honest about the dangers of technology, while being balanced in our approach, and crucially we must communicate a message of innocence for those who are victimized. If young people know their reports will be met with open, non-judgemental and calm ears, they will be far more likely to tell.

Providing a variety of reporting mechanisms for students will increase the likelihood of reports being made of both cyber bullying and e-safety concerns. School counsellors, peer support schemes (if properly run and supervised), a reporting 'box' and online methods can all be useful reporting systems. Similarly, encouraging young people to use external agencies is useful, including reporting to their Internet Service Provider (ISP), mobile phone provider or in the UK to CEOP, the Child

Exploitation and Online Protection Service. In the USA, young people should report directly to their internet or mobile phone service provider, or to the police or other local law enforcement agencies, where they exist. Some schools have found benefit from creating an email address for students to report to, rather than face to face.

Links to Policies and Procedures

However a report comes to light, it is essential that schools act quickly and effectively, implementing the behaviour policy and sanctions for any perpetrators, and providing support to victims. School counselling services, or if deemed necessary, referrals to Child and Adolescent Mental Health Services or Child Protection Services should be offered, ideally with the support of parents. Referrals to other external agencies may be required, for example if the student is experiencing mental health problems, such as depression; severe distress; anxious non-attendance at school; or feelings of suicidal intent. Collating a list of local agencies and support services for ease of reference is a useful exercise, but any such referrals should be made by the designated safeguarding officer for the school, in line with the child protection policy.

It is important to ensure that school policies are consistent and reflect one another, so the whole school community has a reliable, coordinated message. The child protection policy should mention incidents of e-safety, and the e-safety policy (if the school has one in place), should refer the reader to the child protection policy for guidance about dealing with issues that are also a safeguarding concern. Similarly, the anti-bullying and behaviour policies of the school should be cross-referenced, so that parents, students and staff are aware of the school's expectations for behaviour standards, and are aware of the consequences and sanctions for inappropriate behaviour and/or bullying.

Investigating and Recording

Your anti-bullying and e-safety policies should outline how incidents will be investigated and recorded, and make clear whether this is the responsibility of the staff member to whom the incident was reported, or a lead person's role. A clear and consistent strategy should be employed when dealing with each incident to avoid discrepancies, including:

- interviewing all parties involved, including any bystanders

- taking written accounts from students, witnesses or others involved

- confiscating material or taking copies of evidence as necessary (with particular care taken when confiscating materials such as images on mobile phones. This should only be carried out if detailed in the school behaviour policy and if at least one other member of staff is present). In the case of a cyber bullying incident, for example, the school may wish to take a copy of a printed online conversation as evidence

- making referrals and/or employing sanctions as necessary

- making notes in the student's school records as necessary (for example, of sanctions employed)

- informing parents or carers as necessary

- informing other staff members as necessary, such as asking a form tutor to be watchful for further incidents, or asking the child protection officer to make a referral for external support

- creating a system for monitoring with those involved; for example, holding a follow-up meeting with students and parents, or creating an informal system for a victimized student to 'check-in' with a member of staff as necessary.

The methods used to investigate and the consequential steps taken will naturally depend on the nature of the incident reported. A very serious incident of a child being the victim of an online predator and sexual abuse, for example, will be dealt with quite differently from a mild case of teasing via Facebook, with immediate police, parental and external agency involvement as per any incident of child abuse. However, all incidents should be taken seriously and the same process of investigation should apply.

Schools are increasingly employing computer-based record keeping procedures, and this can help staff to identify patterns of behaviour, bullying trends and to invoke more serious consequences, such as exclusion, when a maximum number of sanctions have been given to any one student. For those schools not using technology, it is important to categorize incidents consistently in a child's record. This will also protect schools when taking steps to suspend or exclude a student for extreme or continual poor behaviour – a parent or carer should be able to see clear records of their child's past misdemeanours and/or a clear account of the current incident and process employed by staff to investigate which led to their expulsion.

Monitoring and Review

As with any issue concerning a child's welfare or behaviour, a system of monitoring will ensure the child has received the support he or she needs, is not experiencing repeat victimization, and will ensure that perpetrators have fulfilled their sanctions and are not repeating their transgressions. Monitoring students can take many different forms, from 'soft' or informal monitoring, such as having a chat with a student in the school hallway, or checking in with their form tutor, to more formal processes, such as planned and minuted meetings with staff, students, parents and representatives from local agencies.

In the appendices you will find a sample letter to parents and carers explaining that their child has been involved in an incident of cyber bullying or inappropriate behaviour using technology, which is in violation of the school e-safety policy. You can also adapt this letter to invite parents to monitoring meetings, or to involve external agencies.

Sex and Technology: Responding to Incidents

There is a clear link between young people's use of technology and increasing levels of sexualized behaviour, sexual bullying, sexualization and exploitation. Technologies and platforms such as social networking sites, chat rooms, text messaging and mobile phones with inbuilt cameras make it extremely easy for people to communicate with friends or strangers, and consequently to engage in sexual activity, intentionally and accidentally. The National Society for the Prevention of Cruelty to Children in the UK reports that sexual bullying is a growing problem (NSPCC, 2010). A UK charity, Young Voice, conducted a survey of children and young people's experiences of sexual bullying, revealing that 10 per cent of respondents aged 11–19 had been forced to do something sexual, with 15 per cent experiencing unwanted touching (Young Voice, 2008). In the USA, sexual bullying and harassment in schools is just as much of a concern, and for many teens is a part of everyday school life. Research conducted by the American Association of University Women found that 48 per cent of students surveyed experienced some form of sexual harassment in the school year, with 30 per cent receiving the harassment by technology, including text, email and Facebook (Hill and Kearl, 2011).

Given the rise in sexting and sexualized behaviour by increasingly younger children, there is an added concern that a rise in sexual bullying coupled with more widespread access to technology can create a messy and dangerous potentiality for sexual abuse, harassment and exploitation to fester. With growing numbers of young people uploading nude, provocative or sexualized images online, engaging in sexting, and downloading and viewing pornography, there is an increased likelihood that students' behaviour will lead to bullying, as they become targeted as being promiscuous or branded with a sexually degrading label, such as 'slut' or 'slag', or worse, their images are shared throughout the school community and through the wider web of connectivity to potentially thousands of people. Sexual bullying is serious in and of itself, but can also be the precursor for more dangerous and harmful abuse. Young people can even become the targets for paedophilia in the most serious of cases.

These serious and often extremely distressing instances of bullying, harassment and abuse are likely to become future school issues if they are not already, as technology becomes more widespread and available, and youth continue to develop sexualized and inappropriate behaviour without support or effective sex and relationships education. It is worth considering as a school a process for managing e-safety issues of a sexual nature, such as out of control sexting, cyber bullying of a sexual nature, or young people viewing, sharing or even creating inappropriate images, videos or pornography on school grounds. As with any serious issue of a threat to a child's well-being, child protection procedures should be implemented as deemed necessary, and schools should consider measures to prevent future incidents from occurring, such as awareness-raising sessions about the unacceptability of such behaviour in school, and the long-term consequences for individuals; for example, once an image or video is posted online it can never be retrieved or permanently deleted.

Staff should be extremely wary of demanding to view content on students' phones or other devices, or confiscating images of a sexual nature in any format. Staff should be extremely cautious in their dealings of incidents of a sexual nature, and if in any doubt, should contact the police; for example, refraining from meeting with a student alone to discuss sexually inappropriate behaviour. Although such precautions may seem excessive, being judicious can avoid potentially career-damaging allegations, or further harm from coming to young people. All incidents, investigations and outcomes should always be formally recorded.

Parents or carers should always be informed of any incidents of a sexually inappropriate nature, unless deemed inappropriate as a further child protection concern; for example, if an allegation has been made of sexual abuse perpetrated by a parent or family member. Local agencies and support services can also provide advice and support to assist schools in the prevention and response of incidents involving sexualized behaviour, sexual abuse, harassment, exploitation and technology.

Part II
Curriculum Activities

Curriculum Activities

Schools and families will continue to be plagued with issues and concerns of e-safety until young people are educated to understand the vastly powerful tools they have blanket access to, and are supported to differentiate between positive and negative uses of technology. E-safety curriculum is therefore essential, and helps to build students' self-awareness, emotional literacy, critical thinking skills, safety awareness, and moral, social and personal judgement.

Included within this resource are 20 activities within four themes to explore the key issues of e-safety. The four themes are:

- Communication in the Digital Age

- Being Safe

- Netiquette

- Cyber Bullying.

Activities explore concepts such as whether we can trust all online content, what information is personal and private and therefore shouldn't be shared, how we can chat safely to others online, and what to do if we feel uncomfortable in a chat room or on a social networking site. Activities also explore the impact of 'blanket-friending' – a process of inviting anyone who asks to be a 'friend' or contact on our social networking site, and how we share information when using technology. Finally, the activities explore the specific issue of cyber bullying, defining, exploring and understanding the problem, including how and what to do if an incident were to occur, and how we can all become unwitting bystanders and cyber bullies.

The activities have been designed specifically for high school (secondary) aged young people, but can be easily adapted for use with younger students. Facilitators are advised to set the scene for e-safety lessons by encouraging students to be open and honest in their discussions, while demonstrating respect and following school rules. You may wish to create a class contract in the first session, specifically for reference in these sessions, whereby students identify the 'dos and don'ts' for behaviour to adhere to each lesson. The activities can also be used outside of the classroom, in a group, after school or informal youth setting.

Theme 1
Communication in the Digital Age

Activity 1.1: Why Communicate?

Resources required: *Large sheets of paper; markers.*

Learning objectives: *To explore the methods of communication of the twenty-first century, identifying the positive and negative attributes.*

To explore why people communicate, and how methods of communication may have changed.

Explain to students that in this first e-safety lesson they will begin to explore the different forms of communication people use, and the benefits or dangers of each.

Split the class into smaller groups of approximately five to seven students. Give each group a large sheet of paper and some pens, and ask them to brainstorm as many different forms of communication as they can think of, in five minutes. You may want to help students to get started by suggesting a few modern forms, such as email or text message.

After five minutes or so, come back together as a large group and share answers. Ask students how many of the ideas they had were examples of *modern* communication, or *old-fashioned* communication.

Did anyone put down very old-fashioned modes of communication, such as sending a telegraph, or using a carrier pigeon?!

DISCUSS

- *Why do human beings communicate?*

- *Why don't we use those older forms of communication any more, like the telegraph, or a fax or pager?*

- *Millions of emails and text messages are sent around the world each day. Why do we use these forms of technology so much?*

Activity 1.2: The Benefits of Communication

Resources required: *Worksheet 1: Forms of Communication; sticky labels.*

Learning objectives: *To explore twenty-first century methods of communication, identifying the positive and negative attributes of each.*

To begin to develop students' awareness about how technology can be misused.

Place students into small groups. Using the labels in Worksheet 1: Forms of Communication explain to each group that they should think of as many positives and negatives for each form of communication and write them on to sticky labels, sticking them on to each sheet; for example, 'Email – positive, it is quick and free'; 'Negative – you need to have internet access.'

Ideally, try to distribute two sets of sticky labels in different colours, to easily distinguish positive statements from negative.

Come back together as a full group, and discuss the following points:

DISCUSS

- *Did the positives outweigh the negatives?*

- *Which form of communication would you be most likely to use to:*
  - *ask a friend a question?*
  - *tell your head teacher about an important school issue?*
  - *contact your local newspaper about some fundraising you've completed?*
  - *tell your parents you're going to be home late?*

Activity 1.3: Communication Overload!

Explain to students that they will play a short game about their methods of communication.

Ask students to stand in a horizontal line across the classroom (you may need to move into a larger space for this activity). Students must take one step forward if they agree with the statements they are about to hear. Stress to students that this is just a game, and although they should try to be honest, there are no right or wrong answers.

The statements can be found in Worksheet 2: Communication Overload Statements. When finished, see who has moved the furthest across the room.

DISCUSS

- *Is it a positive thing to be so reliant on technology?*

- *What are the dangers of needing technology in our lives?*

Now ask students to get into pairs, or small groups of three. Give each group a copy of Worksheet 3: True or False? Students should work together to decide whether each statement is true or false. When complete, come back together and share the answers, as follows:

Q1: True. On average, teens watch television for about three hours every day and listen to music or watch music videos for another one to two hours.

Q2: True. Teens spend more than seven and a half hours each day using some form of media or technology.

Q3: False. Teens spend an hour *and a half* each day texting or talking on their phones.

Q4: False. Sixty per cent, not fifty, of teens who have one say they are highly addicted to their Smartphone.

Q5: True. Nine out of ten people own a mobile phone (36% in 2000; 91% in 2011).

Q6: True. The average person sends 50 text messages per week.

Q7: False. Fifty-seven per cent of people talk to more people online than they do in real life.

DISCUSS:

- *Was anyone surprised by the results?*

- *Do the answers match your use of media and technology?*

- *What are the dangers of us not communicating face to face as much with people?*

Activity 1.4: Public or Private?

Resources required: *Worksheet 4: Public or Private?; scissors.*

Learning objectives: *To explore the difference between public and private information, and how private information can easily be shared.*

To explore the potential consequences when private information is publicly shared.

Explain to students that the internet represents a connection to billions of people, all around the world. Unless we are careful, the information we post can potentially be seen by anyone. Lots of people post private information that can then be viewed publicly by everyone. This is not only poor common sense, but also dangerous.

Place students into groups of approximately five to seven and give each group a copy of Worksheet 4: Public or Private? Students should cut up the statements and place them into two columns: one for public information that can be shared with anyone without worry; and one for private information that should not be shared, or should only be shared with trusted people, such as family members.

When complete come back together and read out each label, asking students to tell you if it should be 'public' or 'private'.

DISCUSS

- *Was it difficult to decide which should be public or private?*

- *Has anyone seen someone post a 'private' piece of information online, in a social networking site, for example?*

- *What are the dangers of posting private information for all to see?*

Activity 1.5: Trusting Content

Resources required: *Worksheet 5: Trusting Content.*

Learning objectives: *To build student awareness about the importance of checking the validity of content, particularly that found online.*

To build student awareness that not all content can be trusted.

Explain to students that the internet contains more information than the world's largest library, and is growing all the time. These days anyone can easily add their own information to the internet, which may or may not be inappropriate, dangerous, inaccurate or misleading. When we read or take information from the internet it is our job to check whether it is accurate. We can look in other places to see if the same information is posted there (i.e. find more evidence), ask someone we trust or look offline for the same information – usually printed books are checked much more closely to ensure they are accurate.

Working in small groups, give students a copy of Worksheet 5: Trusting Content, and ask each group to cut up the labels and place them in two columns – content they would trust, and content they wouldn't.

Come back together as a whole group and discuss the following points:

DISCUSS

- *What is it about the content you* don't *trust that makes you doubt it?*

- *What is it about the content you* do *trust that makes you sure you can rely on it?*

- *If you read something online about someone, for example, another student, how do you know it's true?*

- *Do people share information about others, even though they know it might not be true?*

Activity 1.6: Trusting Content Continued

Resources required: *Plain paper (one sheet per student); pens.*

Learning objectives: *To specifically explore whether content on social networking sites can be trusted.*

To begin to identify how easy it is for people to lie or post inaccurate and misleading information online.

Following on from the previous activity, explain to students that they will now create their own profile for a pretend social networking site. Give students a piece of paper and ask them to write a short 'profile' of themselves that they might put on a social networking site. This should only be a few lines long, and should include information about themselves, including:

- hobbies and interests

- favourite music or films

- things they're into

- favourite subjects at school

- information about their family (e.g. how many brothers and sisters)

- goals or dreams for the future

- anything they'd like people to know!

Students should write a paragraph for the profile, and in it hide two lies. For example, they could lie about their hobbies, where they live, or the number of siblings they have. Give students ten minutes to complete their profiles and then gather everyone together in a circle.

Instruct each person to show their profile and read it aloud. The rest of the group have to decide which two pieces of information are lies. When everyone has shared their profile, discuss the following points:

DISCUSS

- *Was it easy for us to guess which people's lies in this class were? Why (i.e. we can see each other face to face, and we know each other pretty well in real life)?*

- *In real life do you think people lie on their profiles or in other ways online? Why?*

- *What are the dangers of not knowing if people are lying about who they are online?*

Theme 2
Being Safe

Activity 2.1: Chat Room Safety

Resources required: *Worksheet 6: Chat Room Case Studies.*

Learning objectives: *To identify the dangers of using online chat rooms, specifically exploring whether strangers can be trusted online.*

To develop an understanding of how easy it can be to give personal and private information over the internet to strangers, and the potential dangers of this.

Discuss with students why and how people chat online. What are the various types of chat rooms or chat functions? (For example, Facebook Chat, Yahoo Chat, chat rooms around themes and topics, such as music or sports). With some forms of chat rooms or platforms users know who they are talking to – for example, talking to a friend using Facebook Chat. Other chat rooms are anonymous and we can only rely on what the person is telling us.

Remind students of what constitutes personal or private information, and why it isn't a good idea to share this with strangers.

Working in small groups, distribute Worksheet 6: Chat Room Case Studies, and ask students to read the studies and answer the questions. Come back together as a full group and discuss the answers.

Now ask students to get into threes to role play. Two people should role play a chat room scenario, with one person playing the role of someone who is not who they say they are. This person should try to get as much private information from their partner as possible, by asking questions as if they both were sitting at a computer. The third person should take notes about what personal and private information is accidentally given.

Ask students to swap around, so that each partner gets a chance to play each role. Come back together as a full group and discuss the following points:

DISCUSS

- *Did anyone share private information with their chat partner?*

- *How difficult was it not to tell your chat partner personal and private information?*

- *Was it easier not to give away private information for the second and third people to have a go at the activity?*

- *For those who did share private information, why did you tell? Sometimes when we're chatting with someone over the internet it can feel as though we know them pretty well. Even if we've never met them in real life, people can be very clever at making us feel as though we know them quite intimately and can trust them.*

Activity 2.2: Are You Safe?

Resources required: *Worksheet 7: Agree/Disagree Labels.*

Learning objectives: *To build student awareness about online behaviour, and the consequences of their virtual actions in real life.*

Explain to students that they will play a game of agree-disagree. This is a game without any right or wrong answers. Place the 'agree' and 'disagree' labels (found in Worksheet 7) at either end of the classroom, with the 'don't know' label in the middle of the room. Read the following statements aloud and ask students to vote with their feet, going to stand next to the label of their choice. Ask students to share their reasoning behind their answers.

STATEMENTS

- *It's OK to chat with someone you don't know online.*

- *If someone requested to be my friend on Facebook I would add them.*

- *It should be a criminal offence to cyber bully or harass someone online.*

- *If I'd been chatting in a chat room with someone who seemed really nice for a few weeks and they asked me which school I went to, I would tell them.*

- *I would go to meet someone I'd met online in real life.*

- *If I received an email from someone I didn't know with an attachment I would open it.*

DISCUSS

As each statement is read discuss students' answers and encourage debate. Use open questions to encourage young people to think about their responses, such as:

- *Would it be safe to meet someone you'd met online, even if you thought you knew them really well?*

- *Are there any potential dangers or risks when adding someone you don't know as a friend on Facebook?*

- *If an attachment on an email contained a virus, what might happen when we opened it?*

Activity 2.3: Trusting Technology

Resources required: *Worksheet 8: Can I Trust U? Case Study.*

Learning objectives: *To explore the difference between public and private information, and how private information can easily be shared.*

To explore the potential consequences when private information is publicly shared.

Split the class into pairs and give each pair a copy of Worksheet 8: Can I Trust U? Case Study. The worksheet explores a scenario between two friends who fall out, with the consequence of a girl forwarding a text message around the school about her friend's sexual exploits. Each pair should spend a few minutes reading the worksheet and answering the questions. Come back together as a whole group and discuss the following points:

DISCUSS

- *Could something like this happen quite easily?*

- *Who is to blame? Should Jenny have sent the text message?*

- *Was Abby a good friend? Should we be able to trust our friends?*

- *What would have been a better course of action for Jenny to take, before the party, at the party and afterwards?*

Activity 2.4: The Consequences of Sexting

Resources required: *Large sheets of paper; markers.*

Learning objectives: *To define, understand and build awareness of the consequences of 'sexting'.*

To explore why people might sext, and the impact of this action.

Explain to the class that being safe online and when using technology doesn't just mean being safe from strangers. We also have to think about being safe and appropriate when using technology with our friends, family and boyfriend or girlfriend.

Increasingly, people use technology to connect with their boyfriend or girlfriend, and this can be both positive and negative. People can stay in touch by texting, email, or find out more about the person by joining their social network. Or technology can turn relationships sour by people feeling forced to sext, share pictures or video, or stalk their partner's every move in their online worlds!

Ask the class what 'sexting' means.

Sexting can be defined as the act of sending sexually explicit messages or photographs, usually between mobile phones.

Ask students to suggest some of the forms of technology that could be used to sext (e.g. mobile phones – text and picture messaging, instant messaging, email, chat rooms, etc.).

DISCUSS

- *Increasingly we're hearing in the news about teens sexting, and some people think it's a big problem. What do you think?*

- *Why are adults concerned about young people sexting?*

- *Should young people be able to sext if they want to?*

- *Do those who sext want to do it, or do some of them feel they have to?*

- *How can sexting get out of hand or cause problems?*

Split students into small groups of around three. Give each group a large sheet of paper and tell them to split it into three sections. One section should read 'At Home', one should read 'At School' and one should read 'For the Individual'. Give the groups 10 to 15 minutes to think about the negative consequences for sexting, and what the consequences might be at school, at home and for the individual; for example, how they'd feel or what they might be thinking. If it helps, give the scenario of a person sending an explicit picture to their boyfriend or girlfriend, who then forwards it on to lots of other people in school.

EXAMPLES

At school – a sexting picture might be spread around the school, teachers might find out; a student might be suspended or excluded.

At home – parents might find out, you might be ashamed, they might ground you.

For the individual – he or she could be embarrassed if everyone found out or saw the picture, feel worthless, not want to go back to school.

Come back together as a full group and share answers.

Activity 2.5: Healthy Relationships versus Sexting

Resources required: *Worksheet 9: Healthy/Unhealthy; Worksheet 10: Images.*

Learning objectives: *To define and understand what constitutes a healthy and unhealthy relationship.*

To identify behaviours that are unhealthy or abusive in a relationship.

To explore the link between sexting and relationships turning sour or abusive.

Following on from the previous activity, explain to students that we will now begin to think about what a healthy romantic relationship might look like.

Split students into groups of three to six and give each group a copy of Worksheet 9: Healthy/Unhealthy. Students should read each label and place them in vertical order from what they think is the most healthy relationship behaviour, down to the least healthy behaviour.

Come back together as a full group and share answers.

DISCUSS

- *Did we all put the labels in the same order? Why/why not?*

- *How would we deal with a situation whereby our partner thought a behaviour, such as sexting, was normal and healthy, but we felt it was unhealthy and made us uncomfortable?*

- *Should we be able to trust our partner?*

- *If we can trust our partner, should we be able to safely tell them how we feel?*

Explain to students that they will now play a game of The Sun Shines On, with a twist.

The Sun Shines On is a simple game to encourage movement and mixing students. Everyone needs to be sat on a chair, with one less chair than there are people. You should stand in the middle as the facilitator to start (you will be without a chair). To start say the statement 'The sun shines on anyone who…' and name something, such as, 'is wearing the colour black', or 'had breakfast this morning', or 'likes to eat pizza'. Each person the statement applies to must quickly get up and find another chair. They can't sit back in the chair they just vacated.

As a twist to the game, explain to students that you are going to give two people a picture (Worksheet 10). As they get up and move in the game, those people should secretly pass the picture on to anyone they choose. Those people then can choose to pass it on secretly again. The pictures can be passed as many times as people want, or they can choose to hold on to them.

At the end of the game (after approximately ten different rounds) ask students to raise their hands if they now have one of the pictures. Are these different people from those who started with the images?

With a show of hands ask students who either saw or passed on one of the pictures. Did anyone see both images? (It is likely that nearly everyone in the circle passed them on, or at least saw the images as they were passed.)

DISCUSS

- *What would happen if those were images of you that you'd sent privately to your boyfriend or girlfriend? How would you feel?*

- *Although this was a game, is it realistic that images could be passed around the class like this, perhaps by text, email or on Facebook?*

- *If this were real life, how many people do you think would have seen those images if we were passing them on electronically?*

- *These images could have been explicit, or could have been of a bullying situation, or just a picture of you looking silly that you'd rather everyone not see. How can we avoid people sharing our pictures?*

Activity 2.6: The Dangers of Sexting

Resources required: *Worksheet 9: Healthy/Unhealthy; Worksheet 11: True or False Quiz.*

Learning objective: *To define abusive behaviour and explore the consequences of online behaviour on relationships and individuals' well-being.*

Remind students what was discussed in the previous activity, and the definition of sexting.

Share with the students that sometimes in relationships people can feel they have to do certain things to make their partner happy and to keep them from cheating or leaving. This can be the reason why some people sext and even why people put up with their partner being abusive or violent.

Ask students what a loving partner and a loving relationship should look and feel like. Write the answers on the board.

- Why do some people feel as though they have to put up with abusive behaviour from a partner?

- How can we help them?

Split students into groups of four to six and give each group a copy of Worksheet 9: Healthy/ Unhealthy again. This time, ask students to work together to put the labels into two columns – examples of abusive behaviour, and not abusive behaviour.

Come back together as a full group and discuss the answers.

In the same groups distribute copies of Worksheet 11: True or False Quiz. Students should decide whether each statement is true or false. When ready, share the answers:

Q1: True. If you send a text to someone on your mobile phone and then you delete it, and they delete it, it can still be retrieved by the phone company in some cases.

Q2: True. If you post a picture online you can never get it back again.

Q3: False. One in three teens say they have received sexually suggestive messages.

Q4: True. You have no control over what happens to a message or picture you text to someone.

Q5: True. Making someone do *anything* they do not want to do is abusive.

DISCUSS

- *Was anyone surprised by the answers? Has this quiz changed anyone's attitudes to sexting now?*

Theme 3
Netiquette

Activity 3.1: What Goes Around, Comes Around

Resources required: *A large sheet of paper; markers.*

Learning objectives: *To define and understand 'netiquette' and identify examples of respectful behaviour online.*

To understand and explore the consequences of not using respectful words or actions online.

Gather students in a circle. Ask students if they know what 'netiquette' means. Netiquette is a fairly new term used to describe etiquette (being respectful and having good manners) when using the internet. Ask students to identify some examples of etiquette in the real world, and examples of netiquette.

Ask students why netiquette is important. Why should people be respectful online?

Ask students for a show of hands as to how many people have a profile on a social networking site, such as Facebook or Twitter. Ask students what they use their profile for. What is the purpose of being on a social networking site? Netiquette is very important when using social networking sites.

Explain to students that they will now play a game pretending they are on Twitter. Twitter is a social networking site where users can add comments in 140 characters or less (a tweet). Explain the rules of the game: one person should start by writing a tweet at the top of a large piece of paper. The rest of the circle should follow suit, either adding a comment beneath, or 're-tweeting' the original comment (repeating it). When everyone has taken part, review what is now written on the paper.

DISCUSS:

- *What are the end results of our Twitter conversation?*

- *How would others feel reading our conversation?*

- *How many people might have seen what we wrote?*

- *There have recently been cases of people being arrested for tweeting threatening or harassing messages. Can anyone think of any examples of celebrities not using netiquette?*

- *Why should celebrities use netiquette? Are we all in the 'public eye' like celebrities when we're online?*

Activity 3.2: Online Image

Resources required: *Worksheet 12: Public Image Case Study.*

Learning objectives: *To define and understand public image and explore how we project our image to the world.*

To identify how online behaviour creates an image of us in the real world, and sends a message to the world that is either positive or negative.

Split students into small groups of four to six and give each group a copy of Worksheet 12: Public Image Case Study. Explain to students that our public image is the image we give of ourselves to the world. It is not just about how we look, but also what we say and do. All these things give the world messages about us which might be positive or negative.

Students should read the case study and sum up what is Katie's public image. Is it positive or negative? How was that image created?

As a full group discuss what Katie's real image might be like. What might she really be like as a person?

DISCUSS

- *Why do people sometimes come across differently online than they do in the real world?*

- *What are the consequences of not being real and true to ourselves?*

- *What do you think your public image is? How is it created?*

- *Can we change our public image, both on and offline? How?*

Activity 3.3: Keeping It Real Online

Resources required: *Worksheet 13: Status Updates; scissors.*

Learning objectives: *To identify the impact of our online behaviour.*

To build awareness about the ease with which we can communicate and share our thoughts online, contrasted with the permanence and lasting impact this can have.

Discuss with students how easy it is to post something online, particularly on social networking sites such as Facebook. Ask students to raise their hands if they have ever:

- posted an angry comment on Facebook

- uploaded a picture of someone to a social networking site

- 'liked' someone's status that was rude or mean about another person

- shared someone else's picture or video online

- tagged someone in a picture the person didn't know had been taken

- written something nasty about someone and then later deleted the post.

DISCUSS

Discuss with students what might be the impact of doing some of these things. Although it takes just a second in real life, it is rarely that easy to reverse our actions.

Split students into groups of four to six and give each group a copy of Worksheet 13: Status Updates. Each group must place the 'status updates' into two columns – appropriate or inappropriate. When complete come back together as a full group.

Discuss who placed which statement in which column. Did we all agree?

Next ask each group to look at their 'appropriate' column and decide whether they want to move the statuses to 'inappropriate' if the following people saw them:

- your grandmother

- your head teacher

- a police officer

- a 50-year-old man

- a six-year-old girl

- your parents.

DISCUSS

Discuss as a whole group the students' reactions to this. The likelihood is that any one of these people, and millions more, could see those statuses if we don't have our privacy settings in place. It is important that we each go home tonight and check our settings so only our friends can see what we post.

Activity 3.4: Respectful Rules

Resources required: *Large sheets of paper; markers.*

Learning objective: *To identify rules for respectful online behaviour.*

Following on from the previous activity, remind students what netiquette means, and recap on some examples of respectful behaviour online and when using technology. Highlight to students that netiquette can extend beyond just the internet and could also apply when sending text messages, picture messages and so forth. Place students in groups of four to six and give each group a large sheet of paper. Ask the groups to identify some Netiquette Rules. These could be useful rules to display by computers in school.

DISCUSS

After ten minutes come back together as a full group and share the rules. You may wish to identify the most common rules or decide as a class which are the best and create a proper Netiquette Rules poster to display around the school.

Activity 3.5: Photo Op!

Resources required: *Computers with internet access (if available).*

Learning objectives: *To explore how digital images can be altered, and the impact of this.*

To identify ways to keep images safe and avoid our pictures getting into the wrong hands.

You will need access to computers and the internet to conduct this activity.

Ask students to say if they have ever uploaded a picture or video to the internet. When we upload a picture or video it may seem like it's our own property that we share with others, but the truth is it becomes the property of anyone who has access and we can never get it back once it is uploaded. It takes only a second for someone to copy and paste, or download it, or even edit the image in any way they like.

Ask students to get into pairs or threes at a computer or laptop. Ask students to find an appropriate picture of young people online, using a search engine, and to use photo editing equipment (if available) or more simple tools that allow for cropping, overwriting text on to the image and so forth, to change the image in some way. They can enhance the image to make it better, or change it in a more negative way, distorting the look of the person, writing something unkind on to the image or making it appear quite different from the original. Remind students to be appropriate and respectful in this activity.

When complete, print off the images and ask each group to share theirs and explain how it was altered.

DISCUSS

- *How easy was it to alter the image?*

- *If you had access to more sophisticated tools, what might you have been able to do to change this image?*

- *Magazines use lots of editing equipment to change images, such as airbrushing. How might someone change an image in a more negative, dangerous way?*

- *What are the consequences of this?*

- *How would you feel if you saw an image of yourself that you know you hadn't posed for, or looking quite different; for example, your head superimposed on to someone else's body?*

- *How can we avoid our images being changed or used by others?*

Theme 4
Cyber Bullying

Activity 4.1: Defining Cyber Bullying

Resources required: *Worksheet 14: Cyber Bullying Case Studies; sticky notes; markers.*

Learning objectives: *To define and understand cyber bullying.*

To identify a range of behaviours that are examples of cyber bullying.

To begin to understand and identify the consequences and impact of cyber bullying.

Discuss with students what a big problem cyber bullying is. Many young people – and adults – can be the victim of cyber bullying. In the technology-filled world we live in it can be difficult to avoid cyber attacks when we are being bullied.

Gather students in a circle and place some sticky notes and pens in the middle of the circle. Ask students to write as many different forms of cyber bullying they can think of, one per sticky note, and place them on a large sheet of paper in the middle of the circle. Students can write forms of cyber bullying and methods used to cyber bully.

As a whole group discuss the answers. How many people have seen someone being cyber bullied online, or know someone who has experience of being cyber bullied? (Avoid using names.)

Place students in small groups of two to four and give each group a copy of Worksheet 14: Cyber Bullying Case Studies. Each group should read the case study and answer the questions below.

DISCUSS EACH GROUP'S ANSWERS

- *How might someone feel if they are cyber bullied?*

- *Is cyber bullying worse than 'normal' bullying, or just as bad?*

Activity 4.2: Is It Cyber Bullying?

Resources required: *Worksheet 15: Cyber Bullying/Not Cyber Bullying Labels; large sheets of paper; markers.*

Learning objectives: *To understand how cyber bullying can differ from more traditional forms.*

To identify our own behaviours that could constitute cyber bullying.

Explain to students that there are some differences between cyber bullying and more 'traditional' forms. Ask students to recap on what might be an example of traditional bullying. Split students into small groups of four to six and give each group a large sheet of paper and some markers. Ask students to list as many differences between cyber and traditional bullying as they can think of.

Come back together as a whole group and discuss each group's answers.

Using the labels in Worksheet 15 explain to students that they will play the agree/disagree game again, this time deciding whether the statement is an example of cyber bullying, not an example of cyber bullying or if they don't know. Students should vote with their feet and go to stand next to the corresponding label.

DISCUSS
Are there examples of cyber bullying?

- *Someone posts a comment on Facebook calling a girl you know a tart. You 'like' their comment and post 'LOL' underneath.*

- *A friend sends you a video of a boy in a younger year being 'happy slapped' (being slapped or attacked while someone is filming it) – you forward it on to someone else.*

- *You take a picture of your friend looking really stupid without them realizing and post it to Facebook, tagging them in it.*

- *Your best friend tweets a comment calling a girl you know fat, ugly and stupid. You re-tweet it.*

- *A group of students have created a hate website about a teacher in your school.*

- *Someone keeps sending you anonymous threatening text messages.*

Activity 4.3: The Bystander Effect

Resources required: *Large sheets of paper; markers; Worksheet 16: Photo of Bullying Victim; sticky notes.*

Learning objectives: *To understand and define the term 'bystander'.*

To identify the ways in which bystanders can help and hinder a bullying situation.

To identify how we can inadvertently become bystanders.

Recap with students the definition of cyber bullying, and discuss some of the methods used to bully others using technology.

Ask students if they know what the term 'bystander' means. Has anyone heard this term before? A bystander is a bit like a witness; someone who sees bullying take place but doesn't necessarily do anything about it. Ask students to share ideas about:

- how a bystander can help in a bullying situation

- how a bystander can make bullying worse.

Split students into small groups of four to six. Give each group a large sheet of paper and some markers. Students should draw a line vertically down the centre of the page. On one side they should write 'support' and on the other side 'don't support'. Read aloud the following scenario and ask students to write down the ways in which they could help and show *support* to the victim in this scenario on one side of the paper, and ways in which they could make the problem worse, *not support* her, or even become a bully themselves, on the other side of the paper.

SCENARIO

A girl you know at school is bullied pretty badly by older students. They laugh at her and make fun of her in the hallways, and sometimes push her to the ground. You were on Facebook last night and saw a link someone posted to a hate website about this girl. You click on the link and see it's been made by one of the older students and contains lots of photos of her that were taken without her realizing, and dozens of comments from students bashing her and making fun of her.

Ask students to share their answers. Discuss the ways in which people make things worse in bullying situations – sometimes without realizing it. Adding a comment to the link on Facebook might have seemed innocent enough, but it is an act of bullying. Discuss with students the different ways we can help people being cyber bullied. They can even be small acts, such as *not* commenting on a link, or writing a comment of support.

Now, ask students to turn their sheet of paper over, and draw another line down the middle with 'support' and 'don't support' on the top. Students should think of as many reasons *why* they *would* support the victim in this scenario, and why they *wouldn't* support the victim, on each side of the paper.

Come back together as a large group and discuss everyone's answers. Is it easier not to support this girl, or to turn a blind eye?

Finally, using Worksheet 16: Photo of Bullying Victim, explain to students that they should spend a few moments thinking about how this person would feel if they were the victim in that scenario and found out the website had been created about them. How would they feel when they saw the pictures of themselves and read the comments?

Stick Resource 16 on a wall in the middle of the classroom and give students some sticky notes to write their answers on. They should stick them on or near the photograph. Students can add as many as they like.

Finally, come back together and read the answers.

DISCUSS

- *What would you do if you were the victim in this scenario?*

- *Sometimes this happens to teachers, whereby students create hate sites. How would a teacher feel? What might be the consequences for the students and the teacher?*

- *Was what the students did a criminal offence?*

Explain to the students that *harassment and inciting hate are indeed criminal offences.*

Activity 4.4: The Bystander Effect Continued

Resources required: *Worksheet 17: Bully, Bystander, Helper Labels.*

Learning objectives: *To identify different types of bystander behaviour.*

To identify the actions of a bully, bystander and helper.

To build awareness of our own behaviour online and when using technology, identifying when we may be bullying or being a bystander in a bullying situation.

Recap on the previous activities, and what is meant by the term bystander. In small groups ask students to discuss and explore the ways in which we can be one of the types of bystander outlined below.

- *Passive bystander* – someone who doesn't fully support the bullying, but doesn't do anything to stop it, either (e.g. just watches, stands around pointing).

- *Pro-active bystander* – someone who supports the victim or tries to help in some way (e.g. showing their disapproval of the bullying, going to get help, sticking up for the victim).

- *Bullying bystander* – someone who makes the bullying worse with their actions or involvement (e.g. laughing or jeering, videoing an incident on their phone, chanting).

You may wish to extend this activity by splitting students into three or six groups and give each group one type of bystander to discuss and then to feed back to the rest of the class.

Remember, sometimes bystanders become bullies themselves – they stop just witnessing what is happening, and start joining in with the bully. *There is often a grey line between being a bullying bystander and becoming a bully.*

Explain to students that in cases of cyber bullying it can sometimes be easy to become a passive or bullying bystander. Tape the labels found in Worksheet 17 to either ends of the room – 'bully' and 'bystander' with the 'helper' label in the middle of the room. Explain to students that you will read aloud some scenarios and they have to decide whether it is an example of someone being a bully, a bystander or a helper.

SCENARIOS

- *Your best friend writes a comment on Facebook saying another student you don't like is gay.*

- *A friend tells you that someone you know is gay. You tweet about it and some of your friends comment and re-tweet it.*

- *Someone sends you a video of an older boy beating up a younger kid. You forward it on to your friend who you know will get a laugh out of it.*

- *Someone in your school has set up a hate site online about a younger girl. You forward the link to the site to her.*

- *Your best friend says he or she wants to play a trick on a friend you don't know. He or she is going to send them a death threat via a text message as a joke – he or she asks to borrow your phone so the friend won't recognize the number.*

Now, explain to students that you will play the game again, this time deciding whether they would *choose to be* a bully, bystander or helper in that scenario. Remember, we all have a choice in how we behave.

DISCUSS THESE SCENARIOS

- *Your best friend writes a comment on Facebook saying another student you don't like is gay. Do you choose to comment also saying you always thought he was gay (bully), do you read the comment but do nothing (bystander) or do you tell the boy and help him (helper)?*

- *Someone sends you a video of a younger student being happy slapped (someone comes and hits him when he doesn't expect it, and videos it). Do you forward it on (bully), watch the video but then delete it (bystander) or report it to a teacher (helper)?*

- *An older student has created a website making fun of one of your teachers. People have posted loads of comments bashing the teacher. Someone sends you the link to the site. Do you go to the site and add your own comments about the teacher (bully), forward the link on to someone else without looking (bystander) tell the person who sent you the link that it's wrong (helper)?*

- *Your best friend tells you that your friendship group is going to play a trick on a girl in your year by texting her pretending to be a boy she likes, to see if she'll fall for it and sext him. They want you to use your phone to send the texts because she doesn't have your number. Do you agree (bully), disagree but let them continue (bystander) or say no and tell the girl immediately what they're planning (helper)?*

Discuss with students how some of these bystander actions might even be bullying. If we know someone is going to do something mean to a person or bully them, are we also being a bully by not taking action to stop it?

Activity 4.5: Facebook Bullying

Resources Required: *Ball of yarn.*

Learning Objectives: *To understand and define the type of bullying that can happen on social networking sites, specifically on Facebook.*

To understand the ease with which bullying can happen online, and the potential consequences.

Ask students to share their opinions on what type of cyber bullying happens most often: many teachers complain that bullying using Facebook is common, and can be difficult to resolve.

Ask for a show of hands as to how many people use Facebook in the class (the chances are, everyone in the room does). What do students use it for?

Gather students in a horizontal line across the length of the room. Explain that they must take one step forward if they can answer yes to your questions.

- How many people have over 50 'friends' on Facebook or another social networking site?

- How many people have over 100 friends?

- Over 150?

- Over 250?

- Over 400?

- Over 600?

- Over 800?

- Over 1000?

See who has moved the furthest across the room.

DISCUSS

- *Do you know all of those people in real life? That is, are they people you have met face to face?*

- *What are the dangers of adding people we don't know to our contacts list on our social networking site?*

- *What do those people have access to on your page (information, status updates, photos, videos)?*

- *Is it safe to add people we don't know?*

Ask each student to share (if they are willing to do so) a rough estimate for how many friends, or contacts, they have on their social networking site. Jot the answers down on the board.

Seat students in a circle, and explain that they will now play a game about Facebook bullying. Holding a ball of yarn, explain that you will start by making a comment about a fictitious student, as if you were writing a status on Facebook. You will then throw the ball of yarn to the next person who wants to 'add' their own comment to yours, as if they were commenting on Facebook. Be sure to hold on to your end of the yarn before you throw the ball.

Continue throwing the ball of yarn to anyone who wants to make a comment – it does not have to be in order of seats in the circle. Encourage students to role play and pretend they are on Facebook, but be appropriate with their language. Students can either make a bullying statement of their own, or a helping comment. As comments are being made, the yarn should begin to create a spider's web effect as the ball is thrown from person to person.

When everyone has had a turn, ask the last person to throw the ball of yarn back to you.

DISCUSS

- *Although we were having a bit of fun with a pretend scenario there, could this sort of thing happen in real life? Does it happen whereby lots of people make nasty comments based on one initial person's comment?*

- *What would happen if I deleted my original comment (teacher)? Would I then look like the bully, or would those who commented look like the bully?*

- *How would the person feel seeing all these comments about them?*

- *Look at the spider's web that has been created with the yarn: we have spread that meanness and bullying all around our social networks.*

Looking at the figures written on the board earlier, make a rough estimate of how many people the class have in their collective networks – potentially thousands and thousands!

- *How does it make us feel for all those people to see us bullying someone online?*

Part III
Worksheets

Forms of Communication

Email

Writing a letter

Text message

Instant messaging

Chat room

Fax

Carrier pigeon

Face to face

Social networking site

Video chat

Communication Overload Statements

- I would be lost without my mobile phone.

- I would look at my phone if it went off in the night and woke me up.

- The first thing I do in the morning is check my phone.

- I would be offended or worried if someone didn't respond to a text message within an hour or two.

- I check my emails daily.

- I check my Facebook or Twitter accounts every time I get my phone out or when I'm by a computer.

- I have more friends on Facebook than I do in real life.

- I take pictures when I'm with friends just so I can post them to Facebook for everyone to see.

- I spend more time speaking to people online or by text than I do face to face.

- I sometimes look at my friends' profiles to see what they're doing and who they're with.

Worksheet 3
True or False?

Read the statements below and decide whether each one is TRUE or FALSE!

1. On average, teens watch television for about three hours every day and listen to music or watch music videos for another one to two hours.

    TRUE   FALSE

2. Teens spend more than seven and a half hours each day using some form of media or technology, including TV, a games console or a computer.

    TRUE   FALSE

3. Teens spend on average an hour each day texting or talking on their phones.

    TRUE   FALSE

4. Fifty per cent of teens who have one say they are highly addicted to their Smartphone (e.g. iPhone or BlackBerry).

    TRUE   FALSE

5. Nine out of ten people own a mobile phone.

    TRUE   FALSE

6. The average person sends 50 text messages per week.

    TRUE   FALSE

7. Forty per cent of people talk to more people online than they do in real life.

    TRUE   FALSE

Public or Private?

First name	Hobby or interests
Last name	The sports team you support
Your school	Your date of birth
Home address	Parent's credit card details
Phone number	City you live in
Email address	Your Twitter handle
Favourite colour	

Worksheet 5
Trusting Content

Which content would you trust, and which would you not? Think about if it's real.

A website you found after a Google search that talks about aliens coming to Earth.

An email you received from enquiries@NationalLottery.com with the subject line 'Winning Ticket'.

A letter from your head teacher, on school headed paper, congratulating you on winning an award recently.

A friend request on Facebook from someone you don't know.

A leaflet that is posted through your door offering discounted sportswear at a local shop.

A text message from the number '87201' saying you have been selected to win a prize to meet your favourite band, if you text back 'YES'.

A letter from your dentist scheduling an appointment.

An email from your favourite shop with news about a sale and a discount code to use online.

An image in a magazine of a perfect looking woman, selling make up.

Chat Room Case Studies

Read the following case studies about using chat rooms, and answer the questions below.

Sally broke her leg and has been off school for the last five weeks. She's been so bored all day with no one to talk to, so has been chatting online in a chat room she found on a website. She started using it as a bit of fun, but lately she can't wait for her parents to leave for work so she can get online and chat. Some of the people on there are a bit weird, but there's one boy who she thinks is really special. They started just chatting off and on, and now speak every day, sometimes for hours on end. He told her yesterday that he thought he was falling in love with her. Sally was so happy – he sounds so perfect. He asked Sally to meet up with him next weekend, and seeing as her leg is almost better, she's agreed.

1. Do you trust this boy? Is Sally making a good decision?

2. What could be the dangers in this situation?

Danny has just moved to a new area and is finding it really difficult to get settled in at his new school. He doesn't have any friends yet and feels really lonely. He loves Xbox games and often plays with people over the internet using his headset. Someone told him about a chat room for Xbox players to share ideas and tips. Danny tries out the site and finds he can chat to some people really well and doesn't feel so lonely any more. They talk about the games he plays and he's got loads of tricks for moving up the levels in his favourite game. But some of the chat makes Danny feel uncomfortable. Someone was talking about sexual stuff and other people were commenting. They were pressuring Danny to join in.

1. Should Danny be concerned in this situation, or is it just harmless fun?

2. What should Danny do in this situation?

AGREE

DISAGREE

DON'T KNOW

Can I Trust U? Case Study

Read the following case study.

Jenny and Abby have been friends for years. Jenny always tells Abby everything, and although they fall out from time to time, they are good friends. On Saturday night Jenny was invited to a party and Abby wasn't. The party was being held at the coolest girl's house in the year above them, and everybody who was anybody would be there! Jenny felt bad that Abby wasn't invited, but thought if she kept quiet about it Abby would never find out.

At the party Jenny starts chatting to an older boy she's liked for ages. She can't believe her luck that he's showing her so much interest! He gets her drinks all the time and spends ages talking and laughing with her. Jenny is pretty sure the drinks are alcoholic, and starts to feel a bit funny, but she doesn't want to look childish in front of the boy she likes so much, so says nothing.

Later on, the boy takes Jenny upstairs, and feeling so drunk she doesn't say no. She doesn't really want to have sex with him but she knows it's what he wants, and if she says no he'll think she's pathetic and will go off with another girl. She figures that this way he's definitely going to be her boyfriend...

Later, Jenny feels quite ashamed and worried about what happened and wishes she hadn't let herself do what he wanted. But she tells herself that now she'll be one of the coolest girls in school because he will be her boyfriend! Maybe it was worth it...

Without thinking she texts her friend Abby to tell her what happened and that she's now got a hot older boyfriend! Abby doesn't respond, but when Jenny gets to school the next day everyone is staring at her and calling her a tart and a slut. Abby must have forwarded on her text message to everyone she knew. Even the boy she likes so much is laughing at her and says he doesn't want to associate with a girl who sleeps around.

Not allowing the person to dress in the way they want to or only in a certain way.

Constantly putting someone down, making them feel bad about themselves – insulting them by calling them fat, ugly, stupid.

Saying to a partner that if they loved you, they would sext with you and send a picture.

Buying flowers or presents for a partner.

Talking about contraceptives, even if you don't plan to have sex any time soon.

Having sex on the first date.

Spending time away from one another; giving each other space.

Demanding they tell you where they're going and with who; checking up on them on Facebook.

Wanting to spend all your free time together.

True or False Quiz

Read the statements below and decide whether each one is TRUE or FALSE!

1. If you send a text to someone on your mobile phone and then you delete it, and they delete it, it can still be retrieved (got back).

    TRUE   FALSE

2. If you post a picture online you can never get it back again.

    TRUE   FALSE

3. Half of all teens say they have received sexually suggestive messages.

    TRUE   FALSE

4. You have no control over what happens to a message or picture you text to someone.

    TRUE   FALSE

5. Making someone send a naked picture of themselves is abusive.

    TRUE   FALSE

Worksheet 12
Public Image Case Study

Katie has 620 friends on Facebook. She posts status updates every day about how much fun she's having and how she doesn't care about school. When school results come out, she brags that she failed all her exams because she wasn't a loser like everyone else who spent hours studying! She posts pictures of herself in bikini tops and mini skirts, and encourages boys to comment on her pictures. She also posts pictures of herself drinking alcohol and looking drunk, and comments on her photos about what a great time she's having and how she loves being drunk and hanging out with older boys. She adds people as contacts on Facebook whether she knows them or not. Most of them are boys.

Katie is often posting pictures that look like she's taken them herself with her mobile phone. She is often wearing lots of makeup. She brags openly on Facebook about what she's done with boys and about how far she's gone. She doesn't seem to have any hobbies or interests.

1. What kind of image is Katie showing through her Facebook profile? How might you describe her if you saw this profile?

2. Is Katie's public image positive or negative? How might her parents or teachers feel reading her profile?

3. What might Katie be like in real life? How might she feel inside?

Read the following Facebook status updates and decide whether they are appropriate or inappropriate.

'Jenny is such a tart – she sleeps around all the time!!!'

'I don't know why some people think they are so much better than the rest of us. Get over yourself!'

'Jono's girlfriend is well hot! I saw the pics last night to prove it! ;) lol'

'Cara Davis got soooooo drunk last night. PMSL, she drank so much she fell over! LMAO!'

'Ugh I hate Mondays, science is first lesson and it's the worst!!!'

'Why do bad things always seem to happen to me?'

'Miss Harding from French is the worst teacher in the world. She is so mean and ugly.'

'Can anyone help me with this week's science homework? I'm really confused...'

'I hate David Jonson – he is a liar and a cheat. Girls beware! He'll cheat on you too!'

Cyber Bullying Case Studies

Read the case studies and answer the questions below.

Michael was a fairly popular boy in his school. He played football and basketball and didn't get into trouble much. He had a steady group of friends in his class and in the football team. One day Michael received a text from a number he didn't know. It read: 'U R such a loser.' Michael was a bit upset but shrugged it off – it was probably someone texting the wrong number. He deleted the message and forgot about it. A few hours later, he received another message: 'Aren't U gonna reply, gay boy?!' This time Michael was worried. He texted back saying 'I think U have the wrong number' but the response he received back said 'No Michael it's meant for U, idiot. We're gonna get you!'

Michael was shaken. He didn't know what to do. Maybe it was just one of his friends messing about? He tried to forget about it but the texts kept coming, even at night when he was at home. The messages got nastier and nastier. One day the message read 'UR DEAD'. Michael was so frightened he didn't want to go to school any more – he didn't trust his friends or other students and withdrew from everyone. He tried switching his phone off but then worried what messages might be waiting. He told his parents he was ill so he could stay in the safety of his house. Michael wondered when this would ever end.

1. What was the impact of the cyber bullying on Michael? How did it make him feel?

2. What should Michael have done in this situation?

Miss Jones was a history teacher. She was a strict teacher who kept students in line, but she was also fair, and was well liked and respected by most students. A group of girls got on particularly well with Miss Jones, and went to her for advice and support when they needed it. Gemma, one of the girls, submitted her history homework and when she got it back she was shocked to see that she had received an F and had failed! She couldn't believe it. Sure, she hadn't really put much effort in, but Miss Jones liked her! She expected the teacher to go easy on her. Gemma was so angry, it was all she could think about. She couldn't believe Miss Jones could do this to her, and now she was going to get into trouble at home for having such a bad mark. That night Gemma went home and created a Facebook page called 'We Hate Miss Jones'. She posted loads of comments about how ugly, mean and horrible the teacher was, and lots of spiteful things about her looks and her personality. Gemma invited lots of students to 'like' the page and soon everyone was joining in.

The next day Gemma was called to the head teacher's office. They had found out about the page. Miss Jones was devastated, especially as she had thought she and Gemma had a good relationship. Gemma felt sick to her stomach. She'd never meant for her to see it...

1. What should Gemma have done instead of starting the Facebook page?

2. How do you think Miss Jones felt when reading all those comments?

Cyber Bullying/Not Cyber Bullying Labels

CYBER BULLYING

NOT CYBER BULLYING

DON'T KNOW

Photo of Bullying Victim

BULLY

BYSTANDER

HELPER

Part IV
Appendices

Model E-Safety Policy

NAME OF SCHOOL – E-SAFETY POLICY

Definition of E-Safety

'E-safety relates to the safe and responsible use of information communication technology (ICT), including computers, the internet, mobile and communication devices and technological tools that are designed to hold, share or receive information; for example, mobile phones, digital cameras and pagers.'

Statement of Intent

[Name of school] is committed to ensuring the welfare of students and all members of the school community, promoting not only academic achievements, but developing students' moral, social and emotional capabilities to create responsible and mature citizens for the future.

With the increase in technology available to students and staff both in and outside of school there is a recognized need to ensure that technologies are being used responsibly, appropriately and safely. This policy outlines [Name of school]'s expectations for the use of school technology by all members of the community, and highlights the school's response to the need to educate and inform students and parents of the potential risks and dangers of the use of technology outside of school.

Copies of this policy and other related policies are available on request from the school office. A parents and carers version is also available.

[Consider whether you wish to create a simplified version of the policy for parents, and possibly for students, also.]

Purpose of Policy

This policy applies to all members of the school community, including students, parents and carers, staff and school governors or school board members. The policy aims to provide the following information:

- what e-safety is and how it relates to [Name of school]

- the acceptable use of technologies in school

- how incidents of the misuse or abuse of technologies will be dealt with

- staff and student Code of Conduct for the use of technology

- how e-safety will be taught across the school

- staff roles and responsibilities in promoting e-safety

- parent and carer roles and responsibilities in promoting e-safety.

The Use of Technology in [Name of School]

[Name of school] recognizes that technology plays an important role in the education of students and in day to day school life. School equipment such as computers, digital cameras and recording equipment offers a wide range of opportunities for the development of skills, and enhances teaching and learning across the curriculum.

The technology available is to be used specifically to enhance the learning process, and is offered to students and staff alike expressly for this purpose. Use of the technology, including the internet, is a privilege and not a right, and is available to those who abide by the school rules and demonstrate a responsible and appropriate manner at all times.

Internet access is widely available across [name of school], and is strictly monitored and filtered to ensure the content displayed is appropriate to the age of students.

The school network coordinator/manager is responsible for the overall security of technology across the school, including ensuring appropriate firewalls and virus protection is in place, in line and with the support of the county/district security procedures and overall county/district ICT security policy.

[You may wish to include or exclude references to county or district policies and procedures.]

Reference to Other Policies

This e-safety policy supersedes the previous school ICT acceptable use policy, and has been written in reference to and compliance with other school policies, such as the school:

- behaviour management policy

- child protection policy

- anti-bullying policy.

[Consider any other policies that may relate to or be influenced by the creation of an e-safety policy. It is important to ensure that policies are cross-referenced and coordinated to ensure a consistent school message.]

Legislative Framework

This policy has been written in line with local and national guidance about e-safety and takes into account the potential for incidents of the misuse of abuse of technology being acts of criminality. The following laws may apply to such incidents:

- The Telecommunications Act 1984

- Malicious Communications Act 1998

- Sexual Offences Act 2003

- Communications Act 2003 (section 127)

- Computer Misuse Act 1990.

[In the USA, laws can vary by state, and federal laws may also apply. It is important to check the most relevant and recent legislation for your state or country, or to avoid mentioning specific laws, you may wish instead to add a blanket statement about various laws relating to e-safety and cyber bullying.

Consider whether or not you wish to include this information – you may feel it is necessary to inform only staff members of the legislation surrounding e-safety and cyber bullying, or that this information needs to be presented within a wider context of exploring the school's involvement in the investigation of incidents and highlighting how to report to external agencies, including the police.]

Teaching and Learning

[Name of school] takes the welfare of students and staff seriously, and recognizes that protecting everyone from potential harm has become a wider issue than addressing the physical dangers presented in the world around us. The physical and emotional safety and well-being of all members of the school community is paramount, and as such [name of school] is including e-safety within the curriculum to educate students on their personal rights and responsibilities when using technology.

The ICT curriculum explores the main aspects of e-safety, is linked to other ICT schemes of work and is returned to whenever students are utilizing ICT equipment. The issue of cyber bullying and personal safety when using technology will be explored within personal social health education, linked to additional schemes of work on anti-bullying, respect and relationships. Further opportunities to explore e-safety will be utilized throughout the academic year, such as during National Anti-Bullying Week/Bullying Prevention Month and on Safer Internet Day in February.

Members of the school council and the school buddy scheme will also be involved in raising awareness of this key issue – members of the school council will engage with staff on publicizing school rules on the use of technology, and in devising information for students outlining the key points of this policy and further information on how to stay safe online and when using technologies. Members of the school buddy scheme will be trained on e-safety and cyber bullying as a part of their annual and ongoing training, to better support vulnerable students and ensure that potential issues of concern or matters of a child protection nature are immediately highlighted and referred to a member of staff.

[Utilizing 'student power' as a method of raising awareness or exerting 'positive peer pressure' can be extremely beneficial, but consider whether this is appropriate for your school and the time available to you. Some schools have asked school councils to create a student-friendly version of important policies, such as e-safety or anti-bullying policies, or to write information that can go in student planners.]

Managing Internet Access

In [name of school] access to the internet is offered purely as a tool for teaching and learning. Therefore, students and staff may access the internet only when appropriate to school-based activities.

Students must only access the internet when given permission by a member of staff and only for curriculum-related activities, such as researching a project or downloading information related to coursework or assignments. Any students found using the internet for other means will be dealt with in accordance with the school behaviour policy.

The school network monitors and filters access to inappropriate content, which aims to mitigate accidental contact with material that is age-inappropriate. However, such filtering is not 100 per cent effective and any breaches of filtering or accidental contact with inappropriate content should be reported to the school network manager immediately.

Access to the internet is strictly not provided for the use of private and personal email accounts, instant messaging accounts or other forms of personal contact or entertainment. Access to social networking sites, such as Facebook and Twitter, is strictly prohibited.

School Email Accounts

Members of staff [and/or] students have access to personal email accounts through the school intranet. Email accounts are monitored by the school network manager and any instances of abuse will be reported to members of the senior leadership team and/or the head teacher. Those found to be abusing or inappropriately using the school email system will have their account suspended.

Students or members of staff found in breach of these rules will be dealt with in accordance with the school behaviour policy and the staff disciplinary policy, respectively.

School Website

The school website is available as a means of communication and promotion of school activities to the wider members of the school community. Information is updated by [name of person] in agreement with relevant parties. Any information to be added to the website should be forwarded to [name]. Other members of staff, parents and carers, and students are strictly prohibited from uploading their own information. Where facilities exist for public commenting on the website, this must be appropriate and respectful.

[If your school website has the capacity for users to upload comments or their own content you should consider how and by whom this is monitored. It is also important to be conscious of displaying images or video of students and staff without their or their guardians consent.]

Publishing Images

Images of students must *not* be uploaded to the internet or school website without a signed consent form from parents or carers to agree to their child being photographed and those images being displayed online and kept electronically. All images must be appropriate and necessary. Under no circumstances must members of staff display images of students on their personal social networking sites or similar personal online websites or pages, and similarly students should under no circumstances take photographs of staff members on their personal cameras or electronic communication devices, such as mobile phones, nor should they upload those images to the internet or forward them onwards electronically.

Managing Other Technologies
Mobile Phones

[Name of school] has a school mobile phone to be used by members of staff when escorting students outside of the school grounds. The member of staff leading the excursion and with the overall responsibility for the students under their care must ensure that the school mobile phone is carried with them at all times, is fully charged and remains in their possession at all times. The phone should be switched on during working hours. Other members of staff are encouraged also to take personal mobile phones when out on excursions in case of emergency.

When on the school grounds, staff are prohibited from using their personal mobile phones when in contact with students, and should reserve the use of phones until scheduled break times or after the school day. Under no circumstances should personal mobile phones be given to students for their use (e.g. to make an emergency phone call). In these circumstances students should be referred to the school office.

Students are prohibited from using their personal mobile phones and related communication devices, such as pagers or PDAs, while in school. [Name of school] would like to encourage parents and carers not to send mobile phones or similar equipment with students to school, as the school cannot be held responsible for any loss or damage.

Digital Cameras

The school holds [X] number of digital cameras which are provided strictly for the use of cataloguing and recording students' work and achievements. Digital cameras should only be used by members of staff, or by students under the guidance of staff. Cameras are not provided for personal use and should remain on the school grounds at all times, unless being used on a school trip or excursion.

Under no circumstances should members of staff use their own personal cameras, including mobile phone cameras, to take images of students or students' work.

Games Consoles and Other Electronic Technology

Games consoles are not permitted to be brought to or used in school, and [name of school] takes no responsibility for the loss or theft of such items. [Name of school] strongly advises parents to discourage their children from bringing such items on to the school grounds. Staff are similarly discouraged from bringing personal technological equipment to school.

All members of staff are provided with a USB pen drive for the storing of electronic data. These USB drives are encrypted and regulated by the school network manager and as such staff are discouraged from using any other form of mass storage device that may breach security measures in place.

Cyber Bullying

Cyber bullying is the repeated harassment, degradation or abuse of another through or with technology. There are seven forms of cyber bullying – via text message, phone call, pictures/videos, email, online chat rooms, social networking sites and via websites in general (e.g. hate or bashing websites).

[Name of school] takes the issue of cyber bullying very seriously. The school anti-bullying policy outlines how incidents of bullying, including cyber bullying, will be dealt with and how students and parents can report incidents.

[Does your anti-bullying policy contain references to cyber bullying? Cyber bullying needs to be detailed with other forms of bullying in the policy, but also needs a discrete section outlining how the school will respond to incidents, what is expected of parents and carers and how issues can be reported. The policy should also mention how the school responds to incidents of cyber bullying against members of staff. You will need to decide as a school how you will respond to incidents of cyber bullying that occur beyond the school gates.]

Authorizing Access

Access to school technology is a privilege and as such, [name of school] expects school equipment to be used responsibly and appropriately. All members of staff are expected to sign the staff Code of Conduct for the use of technology in school, and students are expected to sign and agree to the similar student Code of Conduct, countersigned by their parent or carer.

Incidents of E-Safety

[Name of school] takes incidents of the misuse or abuse of technology, including cyber bullying, very seriously. All members of the school community have a clear role to play in reporting such incidents and working with the school to ensure they are not repeated.

Reporting Incidents – Students and Their Parents and Carers

A student or parent concerned about an act of misuse or abuse of technology should report the incident immediately to a member of staff. Heads of Year or members of the Pastoral Team are available to discuss concerns with students or their parents. Students are also encouraged to report any concerns or worries to a student buddy.

Students and parents can also report incidents online via www.ceop.gov.uk.

Some incidents of the misuse or abuse of technology may be deemed a criminal offence, or be of a highly serious nature that requires immediate police involvement. In these instances parents should contact their local police station or ring 999/911 in an emergency.

Reporting Incidents – Staff

All members of staff have a duty to report any incidents of the misuse or abuse of technology to a member of the senior leadership team. Where staff members are the victims of an abuse of technology, including harassment or cyber bullying, they should save all evidence and present it immediately to a member of the senior leadership team. For serious incidents staff should contact the police at their discretion.

Staff Roles and Responsibilities

Members of staff at [name of school] have a clear and important role to play in the promotion of e-safety across the school. The modelling of positive, safe and responsible use of technology is paramount, and training will be provided to all teaching and support staff to ensure a full and cohesive awareness of e-safety is reached across the school. Members of staff from the ICT [and PSHE] departments are responsible for the teaching of e-safety and curriculum development, in addition to the general roles all staff members play in the promotion of safe and responsible behaviour to all students when using technology.

[Name of school] has appointed an e-safety coordinator in school, who will have overall responsibility for the development of the school-wide approach to e-safety, including organizing sessions for parents, staff training and awareness-raising events for students. Incidents of the misuse or abuse of technology will also be handled by the e-safety coordinator, in partnership with other members of staff. The e-safety coordinator at [name of school] is [name].

Parent and Carer Responsibilities

Parents and carers play an important role in developing children's understanding and awareness of e-safety, and by supporting the school in its endeavours to build students' understanding of how to stay safe when using technology. Parents and carers have a duty to report any incidents affecting students and their schooling to the school to ensure that matters are investigated and dealt with swiftly.

Parents or carers are also required to countersign the student Code of Conduct to ensure that their child has read and understood the school rules in relation to e-safety.

An annual training and awareness-raising event will be held in school for parents and carers to learn more about e-safety and keeping children safe when using technology at home. Information about this event will be sent directly to parents and carers and posted on the school website.

[You should consider to what extent you aim to support parents in their understanding of e-safety. If it is not sustainable on a long-term basis to offer training or awareness-raising events to parents, you should not reference this in your policy. You may wish instead to provide printed material for parents, or promote information on your school website.]

Introducing the Policy

The contents of this policy will come into effect immediately until its review. All staff members will be informed of the contents of the policy and it is their responsibility to ensure that they read and understand its contents. Parents and carers can access copies of this policy from school, and will be informed of the most salient points in the school newsletter.

Students will also be informed of the contents of this policy and a separate student version will be provided to all new and existing students.

School governors or board members will be responsible for agreeing the contents of the policy and ensuring its effective implementation across the school by the head teacher, e-safety coordinator and other relevant parties.

[Consider whether you wish to create a separate student e-safety policy with the most important elements, or use simpler methods instead, such as a student Code of Conduct and posters throughout the school highlighting e-safety rules.]

Monitoring, Evaluation and Review

School governors or board members, in conjunction with the head teacher, members of the senior leadership team and the e-safety coordinator are responsible for the ongoing monitoring and evaluation of the policy, ensuring it is read and understood by all members of the school community, and monitoring the success of e-safety interventions and curriculum through student, parent and staff feedback and surveys. Incidents of the misuse or abuse of technology, including cyber bullying, will also be monitored to gauge the success of the policy implementation year on year.

Given the changing nature of technology in school and in the wider world, this policy will be reviewed annually, with sporadic reviews as necessary such as in the event of new technology being utilized as a teaching and learning tool in school.

[It is advisable that your policy be reviewed and updated if necessary, on an annual basis, given the rapidly changing technologies. Your school should ensure that a member of staff is aware of their duty to update and revise the policy annually, and communicate any changes to the whole school community.]

Date: _____

Date of review: _____

Written by: _____

Approved by: _____

Appendix 2
Sample Staff Code of Conduct

[Name of school] takes the issue of e-safety very seriously, and expects all members of staff to adhere to their professional and ethical responsibilities when utilizing school or personal ICT equipment, and in communication with students, parents and carers, and other members of staff. All members of staff are required to read and sign this Code of Conduct to confirm they have read and understood the school e-safety policy and will specifically adhere to the following points in relation to their own conduct.

- I understand that it is my responsibility to obtain a copy of and read the school e-safety policy.

- I understand that school ICT equipment, including computers, laptops, digital cameras, mobile phones and any other form of information communication technology, is provided by the school for the purposes of teaching and learning, and/or ensuring students' safety.

- I understand that I am not permitted to use any school ICT equipment for my own personal use, including accessing the internet, personal email accounts, social networking sites, etc.

- I understand that I am not permitted to use my personal mobile phone or any handheld ICT device during working hours while teaching or supervising students. I understand that the use of any personal ICT equipment must be limited to specific break times, or before and after the school day.

- I will not install any software or hardware on school ICT equipment without permission.

- I will ensure that all personal data is stored on a school-provided USB key, ensuring data is stored securely.

- I understand that my use of school information systems, including the internet and email, may be subject to monitoring and recording, with or without my knowledge.

- I will only use school digital cameras to take photographs of students, students' work, displays and any other in-school footage, and understand that my own personal digital or mobile cameras are expressly forbidden to be used in school or while on duty as a member of staff (e.g. on school excursions).

- I understand that I am strongly advised not to accept friendship or contact with students or parents/carers on my personal social networking site, and any defamation of students or parents reported to be found on my personal social networking site will be dealt with in accordance with the school disciplinary procedures.

- I will raise awareness of the issue of e-safety with students when appropriate, including whenever students are utilizing ICT in the classroom, to develop a responsible and mature attitude to the use of technology.

Signed: _____   Print name: _____

Role: _____   Department: _____

Date: _____

Appendix 3
Sample Student Code of Conduct

[Name of school] uses a wide variety of tools to enhance teaching and learning, including technology and the internet. All school technology, including computers, laptops, digital cameras, tablets and mobile phones, remains the property of [name of school] and is not for personal or entertainment use. These technologies are provided to teach and help students. Any damage or inappropriate use of school equipment and the internet may result in a loss of privileges or more serious consequences, and may result in access to the technologies being withdrawn for all students.

As with all school equipment there are rules in place to keep both students and staff safe. It is important that students read and understand these rules. Failure to follow the school technology rules will result in disciplinary procedures, in accordance with the behaviour policy.

- I will respect all school computers and other equipment.

- I will not install any programmes on school computers.

- I will not use the internet to cause distress or to bully others.

- I will not post pictures or video to the internet, or otherwise upload content, unless under staff supervision.

- I will not access social networking sites (such as Facebook) during school time on a computer or via a personal device (e.g. mobile phone).

- I will not use my mobile phone during school time.

- I will report any known misuses of technology, including the unacceptable behaviours of others.

- I will keep my computer and email passwords private and will not use other students' passwords.

- I will not make, or attempt to make, any changes to school computer systems and settings.

- I will not use the internet to gain access to materials which are illegal, inappropriate or abusive.

- I am aware that the school has software installed on school computers to monitor student use.

I have read and understand the school e-safety rules.

Signed: _____ (Student) Date: _____

Signed: _____ (Parent) Date: _____

Sample Letter to Parents Re. E-Safety Policy

Dear Parent/Carer,

Re. School E-safety Policy

[Name of school] takes student safety very seriously. This includes protecting students from dangers in both the real and virtual world.

We recognize the importance of including technology in the curriculum to enhance both teaching and learning, and as a part of this process students are offered supervised access to the internet, school computers and other forms of technology. [Name of school] recognizes that students have potentially far greater access to technologies and online dangers at home, or via portable devices, such as mobile phones.

Given the potential for technology to be abused and misused, it is important that staff and students are aware of how to stay safe online and use technology appropriately. This includes not using any form of technology to bully others.

To ensure all members of the school community are aware of their technology responsibilities [name of school] has introduced a new e-safety policy. An abridged copy of the policy is enclosed [or] the policy can be viewed or downloaded via our website at www.yourschoolwebsite.com.

As mentioned in the policy, students are advised against bringing mobile phones or other technologies to schools. Phones should not be used within school time.

The e-safety policy is being implemented to mitigate the risks of students misusing or abusing technology, and it is advisable to consider children's safety when using technologies at home, or when using web-enabled devices, such as Smartphones. The websites www.thinkuknow.com and www. netsmartzkids.org have lots of resources and advice for families.

Yours sincerely,

E-safety coordinator [or] head teacher

Sample Letter to Parents Re. An Incident of the Abuse or Misuse of Technology

Dear Parent/Carer,

Re. Incident of a Breach of the E-Safety Policy

[Name of school] takes student safety and behaviour very seriously, and this extends to the proper safe and responsible use of technologies and the internet.

[Name of school] has a school e-safety policy, which outlines how the school aims to prevent and respond to incidents of the misuse and abuse of technology, including cyber bullying. Such incidents are dealt with in accordance with the school behaviour policy.

It has come to our attention that an incident involving your son/daughter [name] occurred on [date]. It was reported that [insert details of alleged incident].

Your son/daughter has previously received and signed a copy of the school e-safety Code of Conduct, and therefore should be aware of the school rules for the use of both personal and school technology. Incidents of the abuse or deliberate misuse of technology can be criminal offences, and as such may be referred to the police.

[Name of school] would like to assure you that this incident is being fully investigated. We would like to invite you and your son/daughter to a meeting on [date and time] to discuss the alleged incident, as a part of our investigation procedures.

To learn more about [name of school]'s e-safety policy, please visit the school website where a copy can be downloaded.

I look forward to seeing you on [date].

Yours sincerely,

E-safety coordinator [or] head teacher

Appendix 6
Sample Questionnaire for Students

Please read the following questions and answer as honestly as possible.

1. Are you a:

   Boy   Girl

2. Do you own a mobile phone?

   Yes   No

3. How often do you use the internet?

   Every day   A few times a week   Once a week   Once a month

4. If you own a mobile phone, roughly how many text messages do you send each day?

   0–10   11–20   21–30   Over 30

5. Do you have a profile on Facebook?

   Yes   No   Don't know

6. If yes, how often do you use Facebook?

   More than five times a day   Once or twice a day   Hardly ever   Never

7. If you use Facebook, roughly how many friends (contacts) do you have?

   1–100   101–250   251–400   401–600   Over 600

8. If you use the internet at home what room do you use it in?

    Bedroom   Lounge   Office   Other _____

9. What do you use the internet for? *(Tick as many as apply.)*

    Shopping   Listening   Chatting   Watching TV
                       to music

    Blogging   Gaming   School work   Uploading
                                                           content

    Social   Other (please specify)
    networking   Browsing
                                                           _____

10. Have you ever met someone in the real world you only knew online?

    Yes   No   I'd rather not say

11. Have you ever been cyber bullied?

    Yes   No   I'd rather not say   Don't know

12. Would you know what to do if you experienced cyber bullying or saw something that made you uncomfortable online?

    Yes   No   I'd rather not say   Don't know

Thank you for completing this survey!

Sample Questionnaire for Parents

Please read the following questions and answer as honestly as possible.

1. How many children do you have? _____

2. How old is your child/children? _____

3. Does your child have the following: *(Please circle as many options as you wish.)*

Mobile phone	Pager	Laptop	Games console	MP3 music player
Smartphone, e.g. iPhone, BlackBerry	Internet-ready tablet, e.g. iPad	Access to a home computer	Other	

4. How does your child access the internet? *(Please circle as many options as you wish.)*

In school	Home computer	Mobile phone	Through TV	Through a games console

5. How often does your child access the internet?

More than five hours a day	A couple of hours a day	Once a day	A few times a week	Less than once a week

6. Does your child have a profile on a social networking site such as Facebook or Twitter?

Yes	No	Don't know

7. If you have a home computer or laptop, does it have filtering and/or monitoring software (i.e. software that blocks children accessing some websites and content)?

    Yes   No   Don't know

8. Would you describe your technology skills as:

    No skills   Basic/   Average   Advanced   Expert
    at all   beginner

9. Has your child ever been the victim of cyber bullying?

    Yes   No   Don't know

10. Has your child ever accessed inappropriate content online (e.g. adult content)?

    Yes   No   Don't know

11. Has your child ever given out personal information online (e.g. address, phone number)?

    Yes   No   Don't know

12. How concerned are you about your child's safety online and when using technology such as mobile phones?

    Very   Somewhat   Not
    concerned   concerned   concerned
                                         at all

13. Would you like your child to have lessons about how to use the internet and technologies safely?

    Yes   No   Don't know

14. Would you like help, support or information about e-safety?

    Yes   No   Don't know

Thank you for completing this survey!

Appendix 8
Sample Questionnaire for Staff

Please read the following questions and answer as honestly as possible.

1. How would you describe your technology skills?

| No skills at all | Basic/ beginner | Average | Advanced | Expert |

2. Do you own any of the following? *(Please circle as many options as you wish.)*

| Mobile phone | Pager | Laptop | Games console | MP3 music player |

| Smartphone, e.g. iPhone, BlackBerry | Internet-ready tablet, e.g. iPad | A desktop home computer | Other |

3. If you use the internet, how do you usually gain access? *(Please circle as many options as you wish.)*

| In school | Personal laptop | Mobile phone | Through a TV | Through a games console |

| Home computer | Using a tablet, e.g. iPad | Internet café | Other |

4. Do you have a profile on a social networking site such as Facebook, Twitter or LinkedIn?

| Yes | No | Don't know | Rather not say |

5. How often would you say you deal with student incidents of cyber bullying?

Daily	A few times a week	Once a week	A couple of times a month	Rarely or never

6. How often would you say you deal with student incidents of misuse or abuse of technology?

Daily	A few times a week	Once a week	A couple of times a month	Rarely or never

7. Have you ever been the victim of cyber bullying, perpetrated by a student?

Yes	No	Don't know	Rather not say

8. Have you ever been the victim of cyber bullying, perpetrated by another staff member or parent?

Yes	No	Don't know	Rather not say

9. Do you think students should have lessons about how to use the internet and technologies safely?

Yes	No	Don't know

10. Do you think parents should have lessons or support about e-safety and cyber bullying?

Yes	No	Don't know

11. Are you aware of any school rules or policy concerning ICT or e-safety?

Yes	No	Don't know

Thank you for completing this survey!

References

AARP (2010) *Social Media and Technology Use Among Adults 50+.* Washington DC: AARP. Available at http://assets.aarp.org/rgcenter/general/socmedia.pdf, accessed on 3rd June 2012.

Abbott, D.A. (1995) 'Pathological gambling and the family: Practical implications.' *Families in Society 76*, 4, 213–219.

American Psychological Association (2010) *Report of the APA Task Force on the Sexualization of Girls.* Washington DC: APA. Available at www.apa.org/pi/women/programs/girls/report–full.pdf, accessed on 12th December 2011.

Anderson, C., Gentile, D., Milteer, R. and Shifrin, D. (2003) 'The influence of media violence on youth.' *American Psychologist 4*, 3, 81–110.

Association of Teachers and Lecturers (2009) *Fifteen Per Cent of Teachers Have Experienced Cyberbullying.* London: ATL. Available at http://www.atl.org.uk/media–office/media–archive/cyberbullying–survey.asp, accessed on 5th November 2012.

Atkinson, S., Furnell, S. and Phippen, A. (2009*) Using Peer Education to Encourage Safe Online Behaviour.* Plymouth, UK: Centre for Information Security and Network Research, University of Plymouth. Available at http://www.academia.edu/380593/Using_Peer_Education_to_Encourage_Safe_Online_Behaviour, accessed on 9th February 2013.

Barkin, S., Ip, E., Richardson, I., Klinepeter, S., Finch, S. and Kremer, M. (2006) 'Parental media mediation styles for children aged 2 to 11 years.' *Pediatrics Adolescents 160*, 4, 395–401.

BBC (2008) *Is Computer Use Changing Children?* London: BBC. Available at http://news.bbc.co.uk/2/hi/technology/7564152.stm, accessed on 4th March 2012.

Becta (2012) *About the Department.* London: Becta. Available at www.education.gov.uk/aboutdfe/armslengthbodies/a00192537/becta, accessed on 10th January 2012.

Beebe, T., Asche, S., Harrison, P. and Quinlan, K. (2004) 'Heightened vulnerability and increased risk-taking among adolescent chat room users: Results from a statewide school survey.' *Journal of Adolescent Health 35*, 2, 116–123.

Belsey, B. (2004) *Cyberbullying Definition.* Canada: Cyberbullying Canada. Available at www.cyberbullying.ca, accessed on 5th June 2012.

Billmonitor (2011) *The National Billmonitor Mobile Report.* Oxford, UK: Billmonitor. Available at www.guardian.co.uk/technology/2011/apr/11/mobile-phone-users-wasting-5bn?oo=0, accessed on 30th October 2012.

Communications Act (2003) *Section 127.* London: HMSO.

Computer Misuse Act (1990) London: HMSO.

Cooper, M.L. (1995) 'Parental drinking problems and adolescent offspring substance use: Moderating effects of demographic and familial factors.' *Psychology of Addictive Behaviors 9*, 1, 36–52.

Copeland, C.S. (1995) 'Social interactions effects on restrained eating.' *International Journal of Eating Disorders 17*, 1, 97–100.

Cross, E.J., Richardson, B., Douglas, T. and Volkaenal-Flatt, J. (2009) *Virtual Violence: Protecting Children from Cyber-bullying.* London: Beatbullying.

de Haan, J., Duimel, M. and Valkenburg, P. (2007) *National Report for The Netherlands.* Den Haag, NL: Sociaal en cultureel planbureau. Available at www2.lse.ac.uk/media@lse/research/EUKidsOnline/EU%20Kids%20I%20%282006-9%29/EU%20Kids%20Online%20I%20Reports/WP3NationalReportNetherlands.pdf, accessed on 6th November 2012.

DeAngelis, T. (2000) 'Is Internet addiction real?' *Monitor on Psychology 31*, 4, 24–26.

Department for Education (2012) *Principles of E-safety: Mobile and Wi-fi Technologies in Educational Settings.* London: DfE. Available at www.education.gov.uk/schools/pupilsupport/pastoralcare/b00198456/principles-of-e-safety/mobile-and-wi-fi-technologies-in-educational-settings, accessed on 11th January 2012.

Department for Education (2011) *Letting Children Be Children: Report of an Independent Review of the Commercialisation and Sexualisation of Childhood*. London: DfE.

Domestic Violence Resource Centre Victoria (2010) *Eroticising Inequality: Technology, Pornography and Young People*. Victoria, AU: DVRCV. Available at www.dvrcv.org.au/eroticising-inequality, accessed on 5th November 2012.

Family Planning Association (2011) *Sex and Relationships Education*. London: FPA. Available at http://www.fpa.org.uk/media/uploads/aboutus/policy-statements/sre-policy-statement.pdf, accessed on 5th November 2012.

Federal Trade Commission (2010) *Net Cetera: Chatting with Kids about Being Online*. Washington DC: Federal Trade Commission. Available at http://www.onguardonline.gov/sites/default/files/articles/pdf/pdf-0001.pdf, accessed on 13th December 2012.

Fleming, M.J., Greentree, S., Cocotti-Muller, D., Elias, K.A. and Morrison, S. (2006) 'Safety in cyberspace: Adolescents' safety and exposure online.' *Youth Society 38*, 2, 135-142.

Flood, M. (2009) 'The harms of pornography exposure among children and young people.' *Child Abuse Review 18*, 6, 384-400.

Franklin, L. and Cromby, J. (2010) *Everyday Fear: Parenting and Childhood in a Culture of Fear*. Loughborough: Loughborough University. Available at www.inter-disciplinary.net/wp-content/uploads/2009/08/everyday-fear-leanne-franklin.pdf, accessed on 13th June 2012.

Furedi, F. (2006) *Culture of Fear Revisited*. New York: Continuum International Publishing Group.

Furedi, F. (2002) *Paranoid Parenting: Why Ignoring the Experts May be Best for Your Child*. Chicago, IL: Chicago Review Press.

Goleman, D. (1996) *Emotional Intelligence: Why It Can Matter More Than IQ*. London: Bantam Books.

Goldberg, I. (1996) *Internet Addiction Disorder*. New Jersey: Rider University. Available at http://users.rider.edu/~suler/psycyber/supportgp.html, accessed on 4th May 2012.

Greenfield, D. (1999) *Virtual Addiction: Help for Netheads, Cyber Freaks and Those Who Love Them*. Oakland, CA: New Harbinger Publications.

Henry J. Kaiser Foundation (2010) *GENERATION M2 Media in the Lives of 8- to 18-Year-Olds*. Menlo Park, CA: The Kaiser Foundation. Available at http://www.kff.org/entmedia/mh012010pkg.cfm, accessed on 10th August 2012.

Hill, C. and Kearl, H. (2011) *Crossing the Line: Sexual Harassment at School*. Washington DC: American Association of University Women.

Hinduja, S. and Patchin, J.W. (2009) *Bullying Beyond the Schoolyard: Preventing and Responding to Cyberbullying*. Thousand Oaks, CA: Sage Publications.

Home Office (2011) *Crime in England and Wales 2010/11 – Findings from the British Crime Survey and Police Recorded Crime* (2nd Edition). Statistical Bulletin. London: Home Office.

Impett, E.A., Schooler, D. and Tolman, D.L. (2006) 'To be seen and not heard: Femininity ideology and adolescent girls' sexual health.' *Archives of Sexual Behavior 35*, 2, 129–142.

Internet Crime Forum (2000) *Chat Wise, Street Wise: Children and Internet Chat Services*. UK: The Internet Crime Forum IRC sub-group. Available at www.internetcrimeforum.org.uk/chatwise_streetwise.html, accessed on 30th May 2012.

Intersperience Research Limited (2012) *I am My Smartphone*. Cumbria, UK: Intersperience. Available at www.intersperience.com/article_more.asp?art_id=43, accessed on 31st May 2012.

L'Engle, K., Brown, J. and Kenneavy, K. (2006) 'The mass media are an important context for adolescents' sexual behavior.' *Journal of Adolescent Health 38*, 3, pp.186–192.

Kerbs, R. (2008) *Social and Ethical Considerations in Virtual Worlds*. Pomona, CA: California State Polytechnic University. Available at http://www.csupomona.edu/~rwkerbs/papers/kerbs_ADCOG_04.pdf, accessed on 10th May 2012.

Kowalski, R.M., Limber, S.P. and Agatston, P.W. (2008) *Cyber Bullying: Bullying in the Digital Age*. Malden, MA: Blackwell Publishing.

Lenhart, A. (2007) *A Timeline of Teens and Technology*. Washington DC: Pew Internet And American Life. Available at http://www.pewinternet.org/Presentations/2007/A-Timeline-of-Teens-and-Technology.aspx, accessed on 30th June 2012.

Li, Q. and Lambert, D. (2010) *Cyber-Bullying Behaviours*. Calgary: University of Calgary. Available at http://pages.towson.edu/qingli/publication/2012Cyberbully_Li_Lambert.pdf, accessed on 12th July 2011.

Livingstone, S. (2003) *Children's Use of the Internet: Reflections on the Emerging Research Agenda*. London: LSE. Available at http://eprints.lse.ac.uk/415/1/NMS-use-of-internet.pdf, accessed on 1st June 2012.

Malicious Communications Act (1998) London: HMSO.

Mitchell, K., Finkelhar, D. and Wolak, J. (2005) 'Protecting youth online: Family use of filtering and blocking software.' *Child Abuse and Neglect 29*, 7, 753-765.

Musicmetric (2012) *Musicmetric Release Largest BitTorrent Trend Dataset.* London: Musicmetric. Available at www.musicmetric.com/2012/09/musicmetric-release-largest-bittorrent-trend-dataset, accessed on 5th November 2012.

National Association of Schoolmasters Union of Women Teachers (2012) *Don't Be A Victim – Stop Cyberbullying.* London: NAWSUT. Available at www.nasuwt.org.uk/Whatsnew/Campaigns/StopCyberbullying/NASUWT_002654, accessed on 6th November 2012.

NCMEC (National Center for Missing and Exploited Children) (2009) *Policy Statement on Sexting.* Virginia: NCMEC. Available at www.missingkids.com/missingkids/servlet/NewsEventServlet?LanguageCountry=en_USandPageId=4130, accessed on 6th November 2012.

National Society for the Prevention of Cruelty to Children (2010) *Sexual Bullying in Schools, An NSPCC Factsheet.* London: NSPCC. Available at www.nspcc.org.uk/inform/research/questions/sexual_bullying_wda70106.html, accessed on 6th November 2012.

O'Brien, N. and Moules, T. (2010) *The impact of cyber-bullying on young people's mental health.* Cambridge: Anglia Ruskin University.

Ofcom (2011) *A Nation Addicted to Smartphones.* London: Ofcom. Available at http://media.ofcom.org.uk/2011/08/04/a-nation-addicted-to-smartphones, accessed on 30th May 2012.

Ofcom (2010) *UK Children's Media Literacy.* London: Ofcom. Available at http://stakeholders.ofcom.org.uk/binaries/research/media-literacy/ukchildrensml1.pdf, accessed on 29th May 2012.

Ofsted (2012) *Handbook for Inspecting Schools in England under Section 5 of the Education Act 2005 (as amended) from September 2012.* London: Ofsted.

Papadopoulos, L. (2010) *Sexualisation of Young People Review.* London: The Home Office. Available at http://webarchive.nationalarchives.gov.uk/+/homeoffice.gov.uk/documents/sexualisation-young-people.html, accessed on 30th May 2012.

Pew Research Center (2011) *Generations and Their Gadgets.* Washington DC: Pew Research Center. Available at http://pewinternet.org/Reports/2011/Generations-and-gadgets.aspx, accessed on 3rd February 2012.

Pew Research Center (2010) *Social Media and Young Adults.* Washington DC: Pew Research Center. Available at www.pewinternet.org/Reports/2010/Social-Media-and-Young-Adults.aspx, accessed on 30th May 2012.

Pierce, T.A. (2007) 'X-posed on MySpace: A Content Analysis of 'MySpace' Social Networking Sites.' Available at www.calstatela.edu/faculty/sfischo/X-posed_on_%20MySpace.htm, accessed on 9th February 2013.

Prensky, M. (2001) 'Digital natives, digital immigrants.' *On the Horizon 9*, 5, 1-6.

Protection from Harassment Act (1997) London: HMSO.

Public Order Act (1986) London: HMSO.

Robers, S., Zhang, J. and Truman, J. (2012) *Indicators of School Crime and Safety: 2011.* Washington DC: US Department of Justice.

Sexual Offences Act (2003) London: HMSO.

Smith, P., Mahdawi, J., Carvalho, M., Fischer, S., Russell, S., and Tippett, N. (2008) 'Cyberbullying: Its nature and impact in secondary school pupils.' *Journal of Child Psychology and Psychiatry 49*, 4, 376–385.

Smoothwall UK (2011) *e-Safety in Education: A Discussion Document on Standards, Liability and the Implications of Local Control.* Leeds: Smoothwall UK. Available at www.smoothwall.com/whitepaper-library/e-safety-in-education-a-discussion, accessed on 9th February 2013.

Stern, S. (2006) *Girls Gone Wild? I Don't Think So...* Chicago, IL: Spotlight on Digital Media and Learning. Available at http://spotlight.macfound.org/blog/entry/susannah-stern-girls-gone-wild, accessed on 6th November 2012.

The Telecommunications Act (1984) London: HMSO.

United States Code (2012) *Infringement of Copyright, Title 17, Chapter 5, Sections 501 and 506.* Washington DC: United States Code.

United States Code (2009) *Megan Meier Cyberbullying Prevention Act, H.R. 1966, 111th Cong.* Washington DC: United States Code.

United States Code (2008a) *Broadband Data Improvement Act, Section 1492, 110th Cong.* Washington DC: United States Code.

United States Code (2008b) *Protecting Children in the 21st Century Act, Section 49, 110th Cong.* Washington DC: United States Code.

United States Code (2000) *Children's Internet Protection Act, Section 1721, 106th Cong.* Washington DC: United States Code.

United States Department of Education (2010) Key Policy Letters from the Education Secretary and Deputy Secretary. Washington DC: US Department of Education. Available at http://www2.ed.gov/policy/gen/guid/secletter/101215.html, accessed on 12th December 2012.

Valcke, M., Bonte, S., De Wever, B. and Rots, I. (2010) 'Internet parenting styles and the impact on internet use of primary school children.' *Computers and Education 55,* 2, 454-464.

Wang, R., Bianchi, S. and Raley, S. (2005) 'Teenagers' internet use and family rules: A research note.' *Journal of Marriage and Family 67,* 5, 1249–1258.

Ward, L.M. (2004) 'Wading through the stereotypes: Positive and negative associations between media use and Black adolescents' conceptions of self.' *Developmental Psychology 40,* 2, 284-294.

Willard, N. (2007) *Cybersafe Kids, Cyber-savvy Teens: Helping Young People Learn to Use the Internet Safely and Responsibly.* San Francisco, CA: Jossey-Bass.

Young, K.S. (1998) *Caught in the Net: How to Recognize the Signs of Internet Addiction – and a Winning Strategy.* New York: John Wiley and Sons.

Young Voice (2008) *Results of Young Voice Questionnaire.* London: BBC. Available at http://news.bbc.co.uk/1/shared/bsp/hi/pdfs/22_12_08_youngvoice.pdf, accessed on 6th November 2012.

Zwartz, B. (2007) *Sex Acts Copied from Online Porn Sites.* Melbourne: The Age. Available at www.theage.com.au/articles/2007/11/04/1194117879189.html?from=top5, accessed on 6th November 2012.

Index